Oil Painting Medic

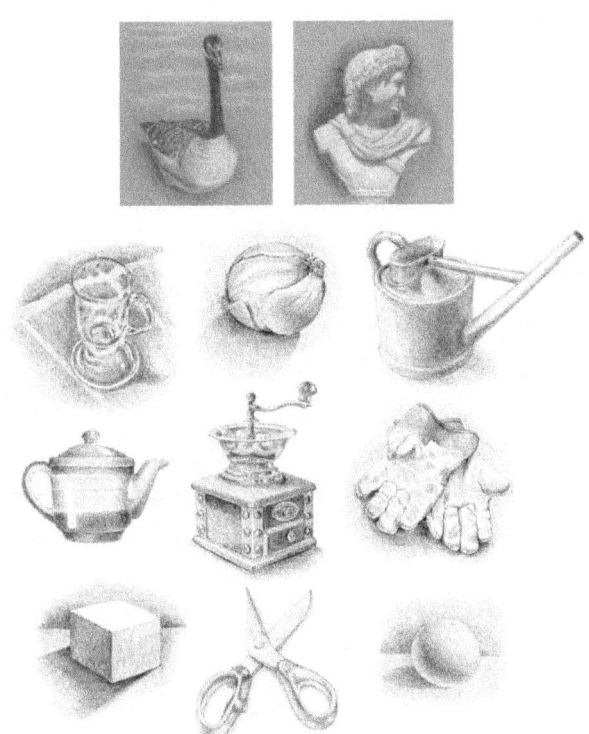

Draw What You See
Not What You Think You See

Rachel Shirley

Oil Painting Medic

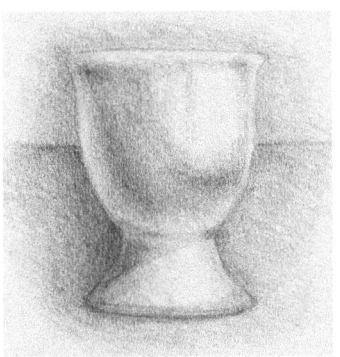

Draw What You See
Not What You Think You See

Rachel Shirley

First Published in 2012 by Rachel Shirley (Createspace edition)

ISBN-13: 978-1475219616
ISBN-10: 147521961X

To my parents Raymond and Sylvia and my sister Heather who inspired me to write this book

Contents

Introduction

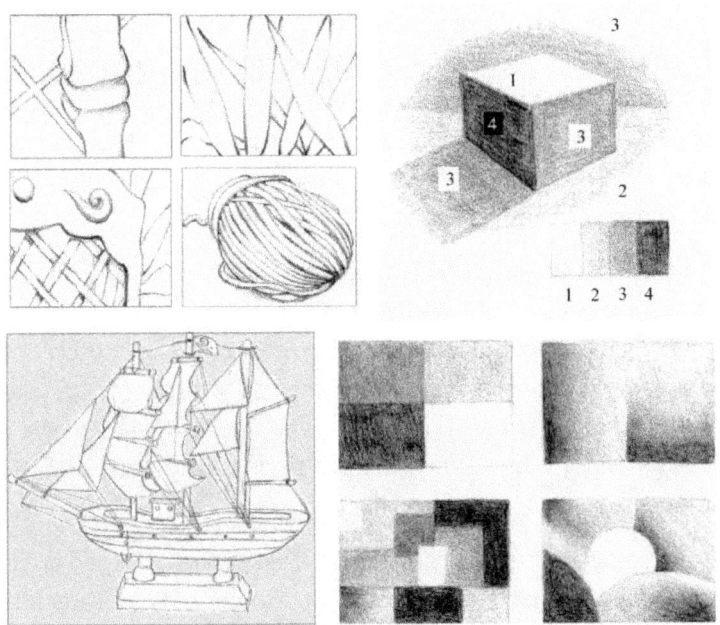

You may have picked up this book because you are at the edge of hope of ever being able to draw. You might be an absolute beginner. You might have spent a lifetime away from creative activities due to work or family commitments and now you cringe at the idea of picking up a pencil. You might be an art student who forever sits apart from others during life class in fear someone might see your work. You might be a child who has a flair for cartoons and doodles only because your attempts at realism are even more cartoonish.

A weary old frustration might descend upon you every time you read about vanishing points, perspectives, plotting and measuring, how everything comprises cuboids, pyramids and spheres. Books proclaiming to be for beginners actually begin with an exercise on drawing shoes or a spider-plant or a street. Basic exercises move on to ever more advanced projects all too abruptly leaving you flagging. Of course, the book is filled with beautiful drawings proving the author can at least draw, even if you can't.

You might be too familiar with books that proclaim you can draw anything so long as you remember the proportions of various subject matter within; the sequence of lines to make up a rabbit, a goat or a horse. And that is on condition your drawing is to feature the subject concerned in certain postures. If only your memory could retain these sequential instructions without continual referral to the book.

Pages of specialised art equipment required for drawing might leave you feeling overwhelmed. Ink washes, pastels, crosshatching and chalk impressions grace your eyes. Different types of paper, special putty rubbers, scalpels, easels and fixatives for charcoal would seem requisite to achieve professional effects. This might be all well and good if only you could put a pencil to paper and be able to draw something – anything that convinces, that comes close to the truth.

Consider the cases of gifted autistic people, who since childhood are able to draw complex subject matter such as the Houses of Parliament, horses and portraits. For the most part, these subjects are unaware of the laws of perspectives, proportions, plotting or have special drawing equipment to hand. They simply sit down and draw instinctively.

For this reason, the main body of this book will contain no mention of perspectives or vanishing points, the use of specialist equipment (except for within chapter 11) or an opening chapter on drawing shoes. I have placed these prescriptive items in chapter 12 at the back of this book should you need to refer to them.

Instead, this book is going to start at the beginning, to learn the language of line from A, B and C.

Within you will find a series of drawing exercises geared towards the absolute beginner as well as some questionnaires designed to decode the underlying causes of your drawing difficulty. This book opens with distorted perception in drawing and the question of how lateral your brain is. This might help shed some light onto my choice for the ensuing exercises.

We will explore symmetrical drawing which exercises all fields of vision, followed by the exploration of abstract forms, negative shapes, the weight of marks and upside-down drawing. Further chapters exercise shading techniques from the most basic practice. Exercises progress gradually onto the shading of various forms.

Opportunities for progression are available in the form of advanced drawing exercises in chapters 10 and 11, including the use of grey paper and soft pencils for shading.

Chapter 12 taps into the orthodox areas of drawing, which are vanishing points, measuring proportions and ellipses. A section on the artist's viewfinder might open out more options for plotting your drawing.

But before embarking upon your journey into drawing, let's get to the bottom of why you cannot (apparently) draw.

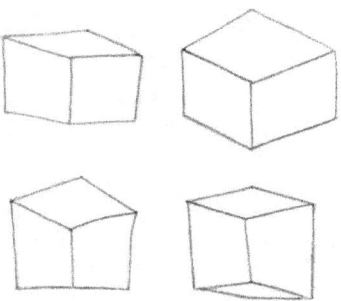

Chapter 1

Distorted Perception in Drawing

Without our conscious awareness, our brains process information in particular ways to help us make sense of the world. Information is filtered, distorted and prioritised. When it comes to visual processing, distorted perceptions can become apparent when drawing what we think is in front of us and yet is not. Take a look at the following images and you will see distorted perception in its purest form.

Regarding the triangle figure, make a visual estimate of where the dot is regarding how high it is. As for the two horizontal lines below, how parallel are they?

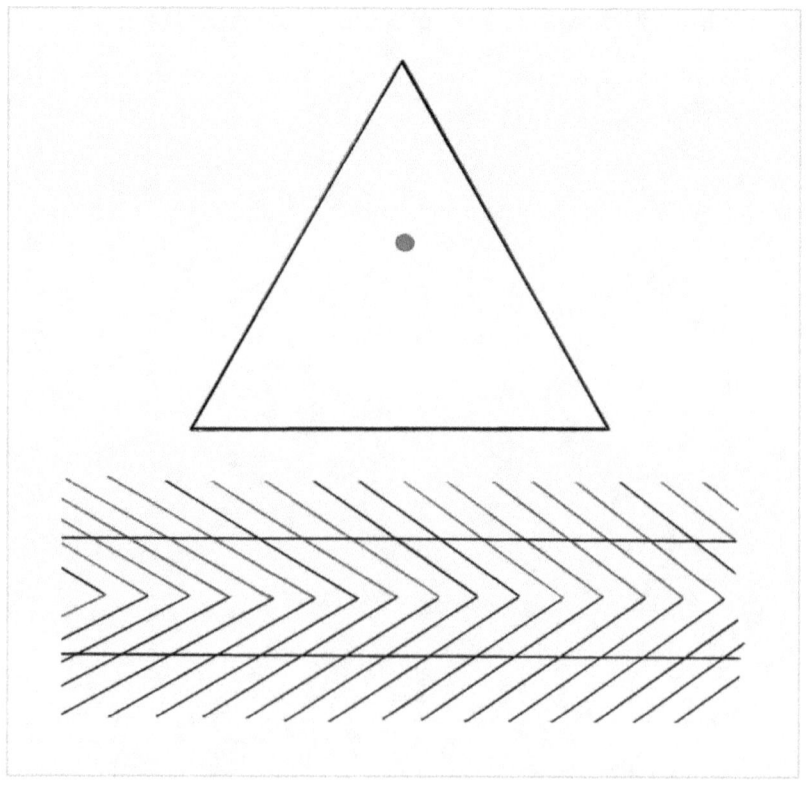

You might be familiar with the perceptual distortions within these images, but if asked, you might candidly believe the dot is closest to the top of the triangle, and be tempted to render the dot likewise in drawing. In fact, the dot is halfway between the top and the bottom.

The two horizontal lines below may appear to converge to the left of the image, but are in fact dead parallel. This distortion is due to the chevrons intersecting the parallel lines. In order to get to the truth, we have to be extra vigilant of these perceptual distortions, particularly when it comes to drawing. Some people are more prone to perceptual distortions than others, and this can be seen in their drawings.

Now let's put your visual judgment to the test. In the following pages, you will find a multiple-choice questionnaire designed to decipher how visually-perceptive you are. You are to choose by eye only (without a ruler or similar aid) which of the four figures in each row is 'perfect.' That is, perfectly symmetrical, or looks most 'right'. Some rows are trickier than others. Award a point for each you get correct. Do not award a point for guesswork. Take no more than five minutes on each page.

The purpose of this exercise is to establish how good you are at making visual judgments. This skill, as you might have guessed, will prove to be an invaluable tool when learning to draw.

Test into Visual Judgment

Visually decipher which is the perfect circle in 1, the perfect cube in 2, the equilateral triangle in 3 and the symmetrical shape in each 4 and 5.

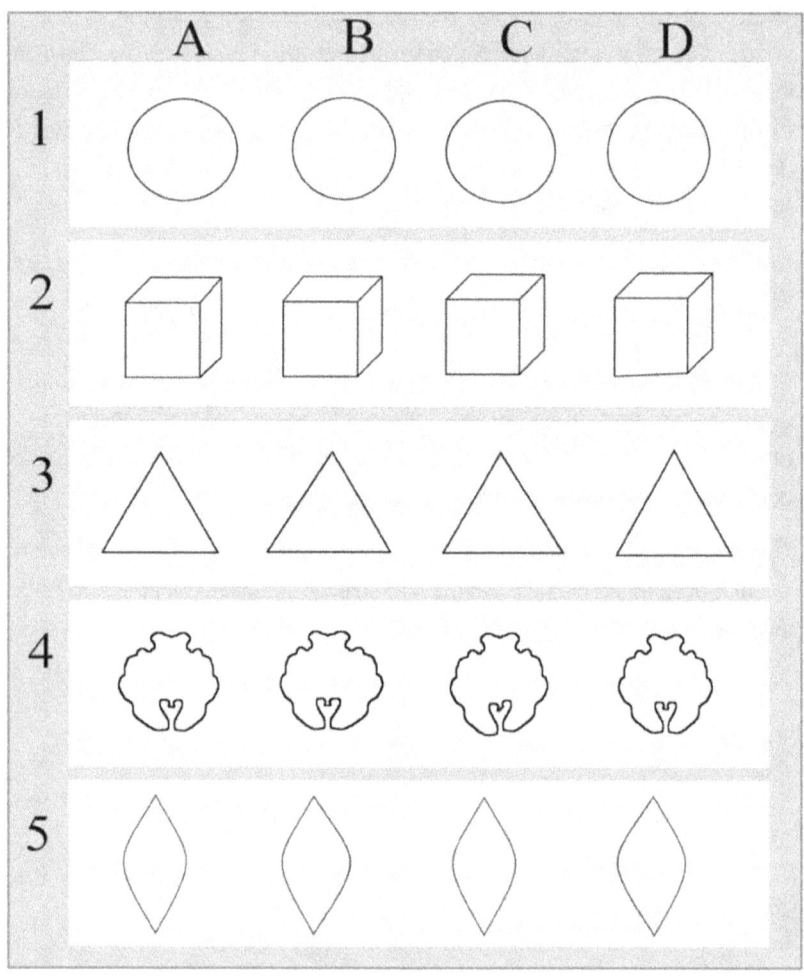

Visually decipher which dot is in the centre of the line in 6, the symmetrical shape in 7, the perfect grid in 8, the flawless prism in 9 and which dot lies halfway up the line in 10. Answers to this test can be found on the following page.

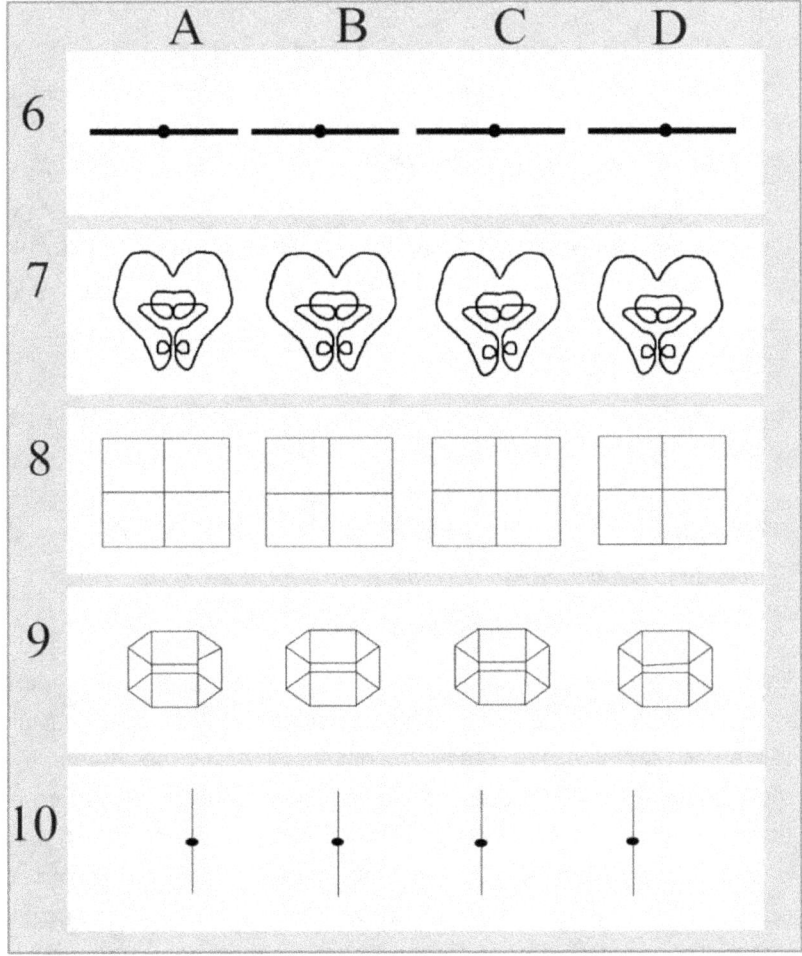

Answers

1B, 2C, 3A, 4D, 5C, 6A, 7A, 8D, 9B and **10C**

If you experienced great difficulty in deciphering the perfect figure in each row, then your visual awareness is in need of development. Anything less than 5 out of 10 may indicate your eyes are prone to deceiving you. Perhaps you find it hard to judge if a painting is hung straight or to aesthetically arrange a bunch of flowers. Don't worry if this has proved to be the case; the exercises within this book are designed to exercise this skill. A score of between 6 and 8 indicates you are quite adept at making visual judgments but there is room for improvement. If you score 9 or 10, then you are halfway there. You just need to learn to put onto paper what your eyes see. Really, this is all what drawing is: making accurate visual judgments and then putting it down onto paper.

The results of this test may have highlighted issues with your visual awareness. It may on the other hand, prove you are finely-tuned with what your eyes see. But correctly selecting the perfect circle is a different matter to actually drawing a complex set of lines that make up a chair or a figure. The question remains, why some people continue to experience such difficulty with drawing whilst others do not.

Picture Blindness

During my teaching, I have come across certain students who really struggled to draw. Renderings would appear small, squashed up, out-of-true and childish in quality. Even a straight line or a circle would seem too much of a challenge. An affliction that can only be described as picture dyslexia seems to get in the way; perception-blindness interferes with what is seen in front and what is rendered in pencil. The most common examples are: objects with impossible vanishing point, heads with small brows, figures with spindly limbs, ellipses with corners and skewed foreshortenings. The drawings do not appear to inhabit three-dimensional space or describe form. It looks just plain "wrong". The question is why is this happening?

Intrigued by what I saw, I decided to conduct some research based upon the research findings of the psycho-biologist Roger W Sperry, whom I shall relate first.

Your Two Brains

In the 1960s, Sperry discovered how the two hemispheres of the brain specialised by performing experiments on patients who had had the corpus callosum removed (a network of nerve fibres that connected both hemispheres of the brain. This procedure helped alleviate the symptoms of severe epilepsy.) The results revealed that each hemisphere had a separate state of consciousness and viewed the world in a different way.

He found that the left hemisphere (that controls the right side of the body) possessed the hard-wiring that enabled us to speak, write, and calculate linear mathematics. The right hemisphere (that controls the left side of the body) was found to be almost mute and incapable of making numerical calculations, (although it could comprehend spacial mathematics, such as geometry.) However, the right-brain is superior in its understanding of three-dimensional space, drawing ability and with seeing the big picture.

One of Sperry's patients was asked to draw simple objects. Despite being naturally right-handed, the patient could not reproduce the images with the right hand (which is controlled by the left hemisphere). He was able to do so with the left hand, since the right-brain understands three-dimensional space and therefore, controls drawing ability.

Sperry delved further into his research by presenting a subject two different words; one shown only to the right eye, another word shown only to the left eye. The patient was only able to verbalise the word that appeared on the right visual field. This was because it had been shown only to the left side of the brain (where the speech centre is located). The right hemisphere cannot speak, so the only way to communicate the other word was for the patient to draw it onto a piece of paper or to pick it out from a box of objects.

Sperry's discovery that the speech centre (Broca's Area), logic and reasoning resided in the left-brain, and that drawing ability, spacial awareness and holistic perception resided in the right-brain earned him a Nobel Prize in 1981.

Disrupting the Left-brain

The Channel 5 program, '*My Brilliant Brain*', which was broadcast on 23 July 2007, provided further illumination on the subject of drawing ability. The theory regarding the talent of certain autistic people is that during gestation in the womb, high levels of testosterone in the blood damages the left hemisphere of the brain. This liberates the right brain-from the left-brain. The right-brain then takes on some of the tasks of the left-brain, creating the talent.

Professor Alan Sneider, who was featured in the programme, performed an experiment, which involved sending magnetic impulses to the left-brain of an ordinary subject for 15 minutes. This disinhibits the right-brain. Before and after the treatment, improvement can be seen in the rendering of a horse. It would appear that drawing ability really could be improved by subduing the left-brain.

Where Drawing Ability Resides

Your brain, then, is in fact two brains which perceive the world in opposing ways – a double view. Although similar in appearance, each hemisphere has a different function: one sees the world as it really is, the other filters the world out, to try to make sense of it.

This 'left-brain' and 'right-brain' are known by various synonyms. Respectively, these are: male brain and female brain, the major hemisphere and the minor hemisphere, the sequential thinker and the holistic thinker, the inchworm and the grasshopper, the logical brain and the creative brain, the dominant brain and the recessive brain, the artist and the thinker.

The right-brain is intuitive, instinctive, irrational, silent, emotional, latent, creative, makes associations, sees things as a whole, is easily overruled by the left-brain and is concerned with thought.

The left-brain is analytical, logical, rational, dictatorial, insistent, stereotyping, bossy, critical, temporal, sees things in its parts, relies on memory, assigns labels and is concerned with speech.

As Sperry discovered language is located in the left side of the brain, an object perceived will be assigned a label via this part of the brain. The right-brain doesn't assign labels. It remains silent, and instead perceives the object as simply a series of shapes.

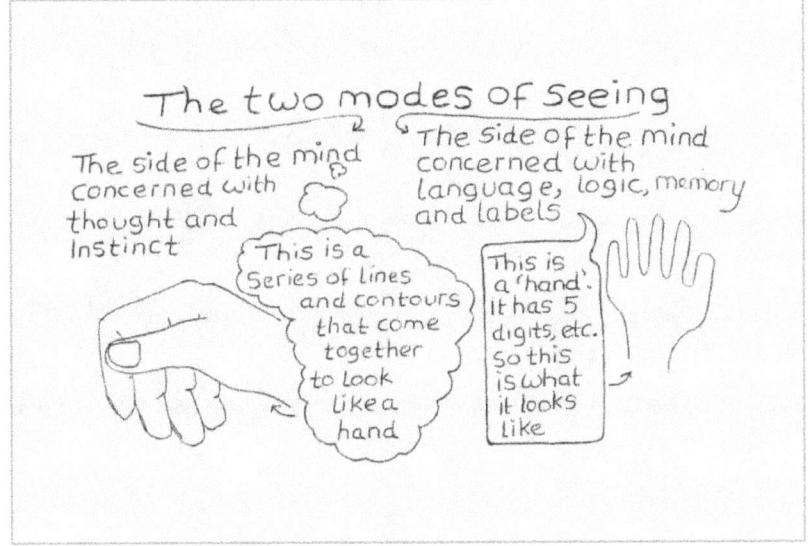

So, when it comes to drawing a chair, the left-brain likes to air its views, such as the following: this is a chair, all chairs have four legs, all have legs of equal length, all chairs have a seat, and all chairs are symmetrical in shape. These features define all chairs and that is what should be reflected on paper.

But in contrast, here is the right-brain's viewpoint: a chair can look like anything. Some have two, three or one leg. Some don't have a seat, some are asymmetrical. By the way, what is a chair? And on that point, what is a leg and what is a seat?

Because of its tendency to categorise things, the left-brain also perceives objects as symbols; generalisations of what things 'should' look like. These

17

symbols can sneak into our drawing in the most subtle ways, sabotaging our efforts to draw. In its purest form, here are some examples of symbolic drawings.

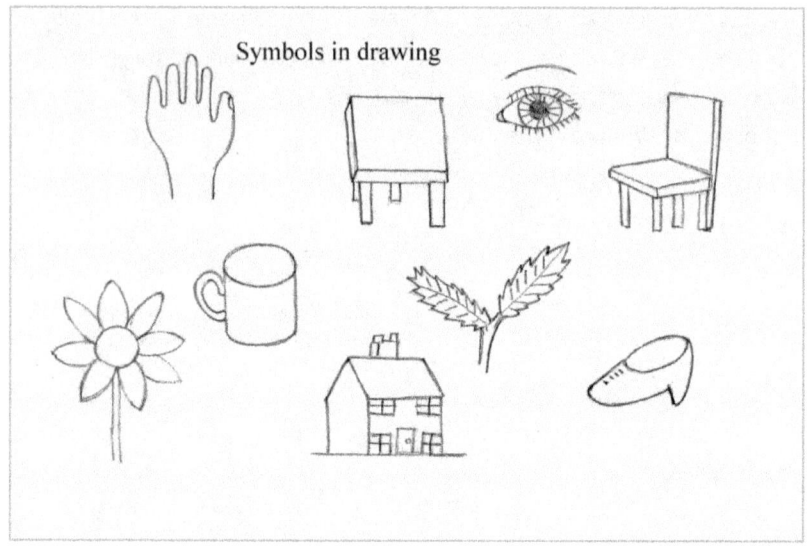

Symbols in drawing

It will soon become apparent that in order to draw well, we must learn to subdue this overbearing left-brain and allow the right-brain to take precedence.

An Experiment into Drawing Ability

On this premise, I conducted an experiment based on the hypothesis drawn from Sperry's findings in order to find a way to help the picture-dyslexic subjects within my drawing class.

My hypothesis was this: if drawing ability really was located in the right side of the brain, could people who were mostly 'left-sided' (that is left-handed, hold the phone to the left ear, use the left leg to kick a ball with, etc.) have a natural flair for drawing or indeed exhibit keen visual judgment? This would appear to fit the general belief that there are disproportionately more left-handed artists than there are right-handed (although such a statement can be hard to quantify).

To test this theory, I devised a questionnaire and a drawing test (see next page). The results enabled me to categorise people into those who performed functions mostly right-sidedly and those who performed functions mostly with the left side of the body. There was a third category: people who performed tasks pretty-well evenly-spread over either side of the body, and which I termed 'bilateral' (not to be confused with ambidextrous, which pertains only to writing).

I researched around 150 people and what I discovered was not what I had expected. In fact, drawing ability seemed (almost) evenly ratioed between right-siders and left-siders (although I had less data from the latter). Those who had problems with drawing were most often to be found within the third category: those who performed tasks mostly bilaterally. In the same way I found, the highly 'lateral' group (especially right-sided people) more likely to render an accurate drawing, or at least exhibit good hand-to-eye coordination.

I delved further and discovered that 'handedness' is peculiar to man. Since we have evolved specialised skills, such as tool-making, writing and language, we have therefore also evolved highly-specialised brain cells that occupy a particular hemisphere. This can be seen in the speech-centre of the brain, which is normally located within the left hemisphere. Could this explain why some bilaterally-functioning people are more likely to experience difficulties with drawing, as shown in my research?

A Dilemma with Drawing

Consider the multiple choice questionnaire into visual awareness you had completed earlier. Did you feel that a specialised skill was required to get the questions right? If so, this might suggest a highly-specialised set of cells within the brain are being engaged during the task.

Of course, more research is required into my findings and not all subjects will fit into the categories suggested. Some people may have difficulty drawing simply through lack of practice or confidence rather than through a particular cerebral lateralisation. But, those who suffer from picture dyslexia may experience some interference between the two hemispheres of the brain. Little surprise rendering an object in a drawing becomes so difficult!

So let's see how lateral you are when it comes to performing tasks. I have included my questionnaire and a drawing test for you to try. Do not include data affected by environmental factors such as injuries, a disability or equipment setup (you may add notes to part E to this effect). Perform the task without thinking and then tick each box. Afterwards, you will find a guide on how to interpret the results.

Questionnaire into Drawing Ability

Part A: Try to draw the following images in freehand in pen, taking no more than 5 minutes in total.

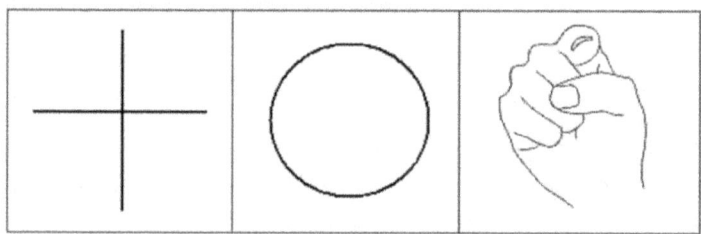

Part B

Which hand do you normally write with?	L	Either	R
Clasp your hands so that your fingers interlock. Which thumb rests on top?	L	Either	R
When crossing your legs, which leg rests on top?	L	Either	R
When crossing your arms, which arm rests on top?	L	Either	R
When viewing through a telescope, which eye do you use?	L	Either	R
When listening on the telephone, which ear do you hold the earpiece to?	L	Either	R
Which foot do you kick a ball with?	L	Either	R
Which hand do you comb your hair with?	L	Either	R
Which hand do you use when hitting with a bat?	L	Either	R

Which hand do you feed yourself with?	L	Either	R
Which hand do you hold a cup with?	L	Either	R
Which foot would you prefer to balance on?	L	Either	R
Which hand do you hold out to greet with?	L	Either	R

Part C

Do you sometimes confuse left from right?	Y	Slightly	N
Do you sometimes have difficulty reading an analogue clock?	Y	Slightly	N
Do you ever have problems with spelling or getting letters back to front?	Y	Slightly	N

Part D

When reading text with illustrations, do you find yourself distracted by the images?	Often	At times	Seldom/ never
When reading, do you have to read the sentence or paragraph again to grasp its meaning>	Often	At times	Seldom/ never
Do you often have trouble remembering words (the tip of the tongue syndrome)	Often	At times	Seldom/ never
Do you often find yourself tuning in to background music during conversations?	Often	At times	Seldom/ never
When listening to music, which is most memorable to you?	Melody	Equally	Lyrics
When meeting people which do you remember best?	Faces	Equally	Names

Part E

Extra comments (external factors that may affect the result)

Interpreting the Results

The purpose of the questionnaire is to determine the degree to which you perform tasks laterally. Are you 'highly-lateral' or mostly 'bilateral'? For ease, I have provided the following terminology and definitions.

Highly-lateral: those individuals who have a strong preference in using one side of the body for performing tasks, and who therefore demonstrate significant dominance of one hemisphere of the brain in this regard.

Bilateral: those individuals who demonstrate a fair mix of task-performance via either side of the body and who therefore demonstrate no significant dominance of one hemisphere of the brain in this regard.

Sinistral: a left-handed person.

Dextral: a right-handed person.

Ambidextrous: A person who favors no particular hand for writing tasks.

The Highly-lateral Category

The following results are what might be indicative of a highly-lateralised brain function regarding the scores within part B of the questionnaire.

Left-sided sinistrals. These left-handers perform 3 tasks or less with the right side of the body and an insignificant number of tasks ambidextrously (2 or less).

Right-sided dextrals. These right-handers perform 3 tasks or less with the left side of the body and an insignificant number of tasks ambidextrously (2 or less).

Highly-lateralised ambidextrals: These ambidextrous people perform most tasks with one side of the body (with 2 or less exceptions).

Answering mostly 'no' within part C of the questionnaire further indicates your brain is highly-lateralised regarding the functions described.

Answering 'often' within part D of the questionnaire indicates the non-verbal side of the brain commandeers during most situations (the right-side). This is the part of the brain you need to tap into when learning to draw.

The Predominantly Bilateral Category

The following results would indicate your brain is not highly-lateralised regarding the functions described, that is, everyday tasks are performed with little preference either way. Again, part B of the questionnaire is referred to here.

Right-sided sinistrals. These left-handers perform 4 or more tasks with the right-side of the body, with some ambidextrously.

Left-sided dextrals. These right-handers perform 4 or more tasks with the left-side of the body, with some ambidextrously.

An ambidextrous subject, using either hand for writing tasks and who demonstrates significant use of either side of the body for performing tasks.

Answering at least one 'yes' or 'sometimes' within part C of the questionnaire further indicates your brain is not highly-lateralised regarding the functions described.

Answering mostly 'seldom' or 'never' within part D of the questionnaire might indicate the left-brain commandeers during the situations described. This is the part of the brain that needs to be subdued during drawing activities. A likelihood to remember names over faces or lyrics over melodies further indicates a domineering left-brain.

It must be noted here, that a sinistral (left-hander) or an ambidextrous person is more likely to suffer dyslexia and directional issues than a right-handed person (DfES, Access for All: 2007).

Now to part A. How did your fare with drawing the cross and the circle? A significant asymmetry in rendering these images could indicate poor coordination and visual judgment. Examples are if the circle is elliptical or flattened at one side or if the lines of the cross are not perpendicular or centered within the box. If you have low drawing ability, you might be tempted to try to illustrate the length of the pointing finger. The hand might otherwise exhibit spindly fingers or of the wrong proportions. Drawing an object in foreshortening is a classic way of exposing a domineering left-brain. In such a case, basic drawing exercises are certainly needed.

Of course, this questionnaire serves as a basic guide. The brain is more complex than the results might imply, but it certainly helps give an idea of how your brain is specialised when it comes to drawing and offer some insight into how the exercises within this book might help improve your drawing ability.

Now to explore the language of line from the beginning.

Chapter 2

The A, B and C of Drawing

You might have learned from the questionnaires in the previous chapter that your visual perception needs fine-tuning and/or your brain is rather bilateral in tendency. Either could interfere with your ability to draw accurately. You might on the other hand discover your brain is highly-lateralised and/or your visual awareness is accurate. Your only problem is a severe inner-critic and with confidence.

Whatever the result, we shall start to exercise your visual judgment and your hand-to-eye coordination. The great thing is, you will require no special utensils to do so, merely:

A medium-soft pencil; 2B to 4B (I used 4B for all the drawings in this book). Pencils in the H range I find are too hard and are likely to damage the surface of the paper. Anything softer than 5B tends to wear down too quickly and break during the sharpening process.

A pencil sharpener. A scalpel might serve better if using pastel pencils as described in chapter 11.

An eraser (it's not a sin). Invest in a good quality plastic eraser that does not leave smudgy marks after rubbing out unwanted marks. Old erasers tend to harden.

Good quality white paper (not print paper as this is too thin). An average sketchbook offers page thickness of around 150gsm. Hot-pressed paper provides a smooth surface which is ideal for rendering detail. Don't work bigger than A4 in size at this stage. I have used an A5 sketchbook for the drawings in this book.

You will also need a firm surface on which to rest your paper.

A hand-mirror.

And a ruler.

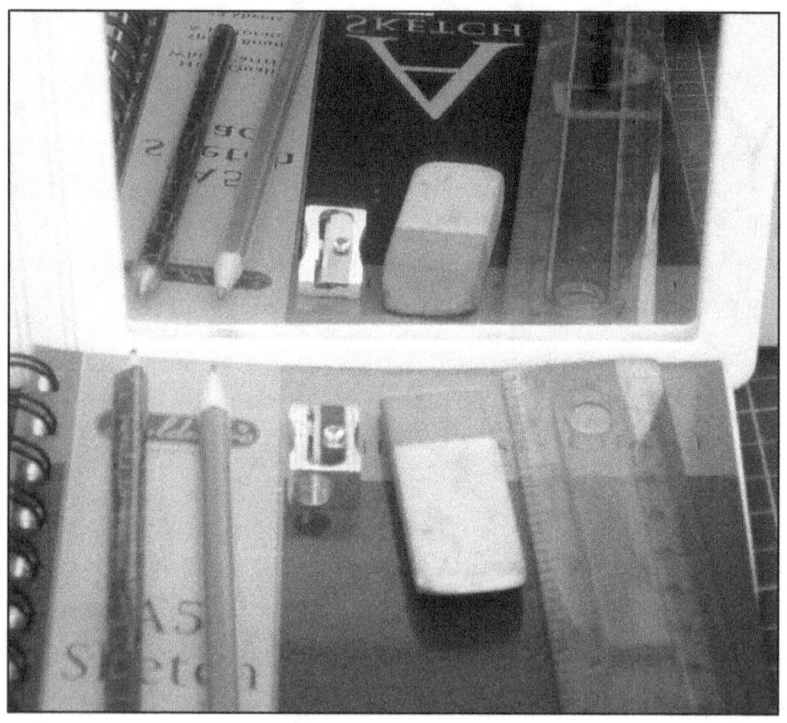

Chapter 11 explores the use of grey paper and soft pastels if you wish to have a go at special shading techniques later.

For now, learning a new skill (or improving on an old skill) is meaningless without some way of measuring improvement. This means producing a preliminary drawing to see where you are 'at.'

On the following page, you will find a line drawing of a ship. You are to copy as faithfully as you can the drawing. It is important not to self-criticise, judge or feel embarrassed about the result. Simply draw and then put into a concealed place until instructed to take another look later within this book.

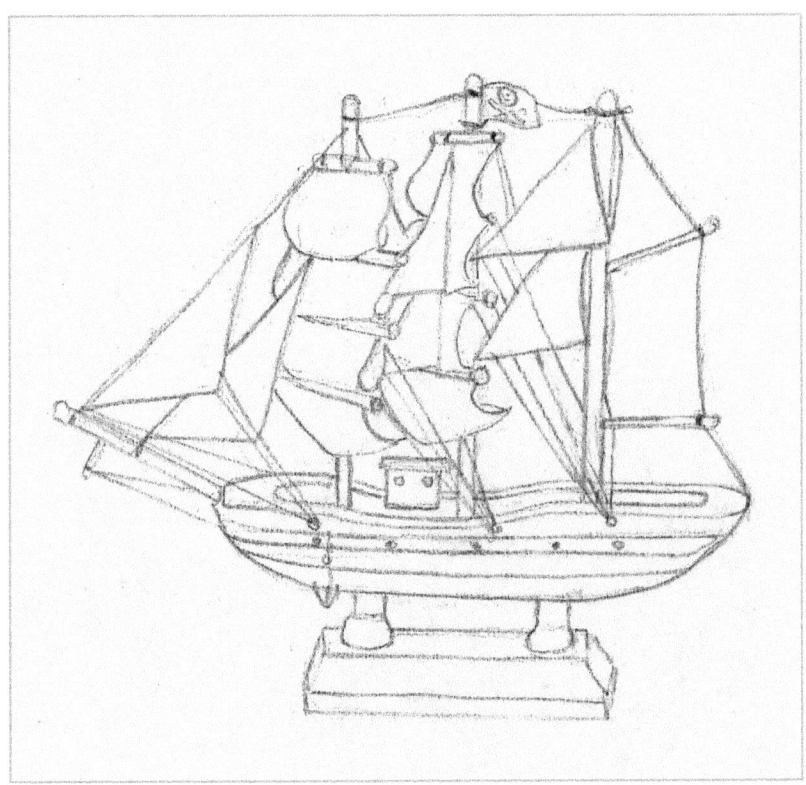

Before beginning with the first drawing exercises, I shall outline a few practices that will enhance the results of your drawings and which will be referred to throughout this book.

1 Draw with ease. If you are an absolute beginner, here is a rough guide on how to position yourself for drawing. Firstly, hold the drawing paper slightly angled towards you. If you draw with the paper lying flat, you will get only a flattened view of the drawing. Hold the drawing parallel to your vision to obtain a view of how it would appear if hung upright on a wall.

Lightly hold the pencil as though to write something and then maintain a light pressure throughout the initial stages of the drawing. Holding the pencil at an angle of between 30 and 45 degrees might be most suitable, or what feels most comfortable to you. Don't press the nib down too hard and don't hold the pencil upright to the page. Experiment with different mark-making. Use the edge of the pencil to attain soft lines. Use the nib head-on to produce harsh lines. Try moving the pencil in different directions as shown in the image in order to get a feel for this medium.

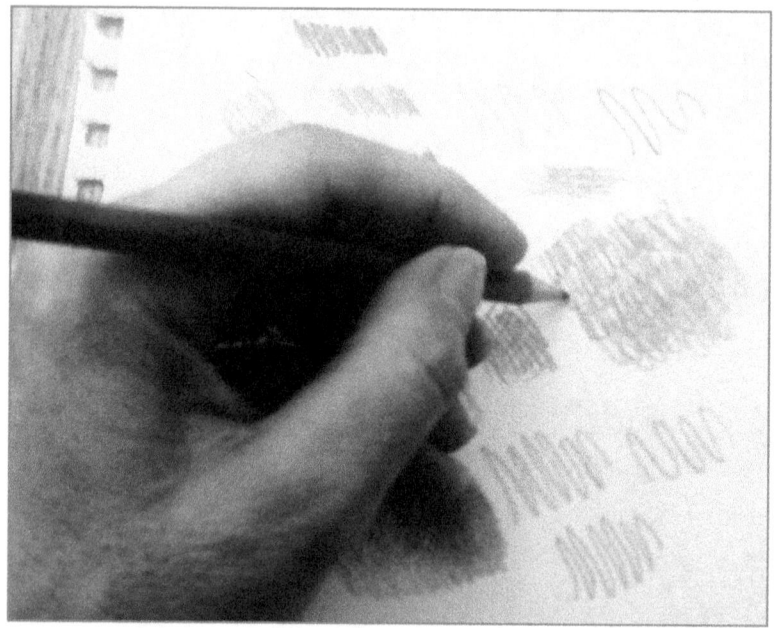

2 **The first line of your drawing will never be 100% accurate**. It is impossible. Even the great artists cannot draw faithfully without adjusting, without rubbing out or without making amendments of some kind between start and finish. Drawing entails making visual estimates and *then* working towards accuracy. This often entails conducting an internal dialogue, such as: 'This line is *roughly* in the middle,' or 'that curve is *roughly* S shaped.' Roughly, but almost is the key. Accept the first line will never be 100% accurate, but that this accuracy can be worked towards as the drawing progresses.

3 **Start light and work darker**. Make light, tentative marks at first. Work a little darker as the drawing progresses and you are confident the lines are reasonably accurate. Execute your preliminary lines sketchy, loose, not

tight and dark. Don't press the nib of the pencil hard on the paper. Above all, don't execute beautiful detail and shading whilst the drawing's accuracy is still in question. What could be worse than a wonky depiction of a suspension bridge that is beautifully-shaded and adorned with detail? Work light at first. Work darker and into detail later.

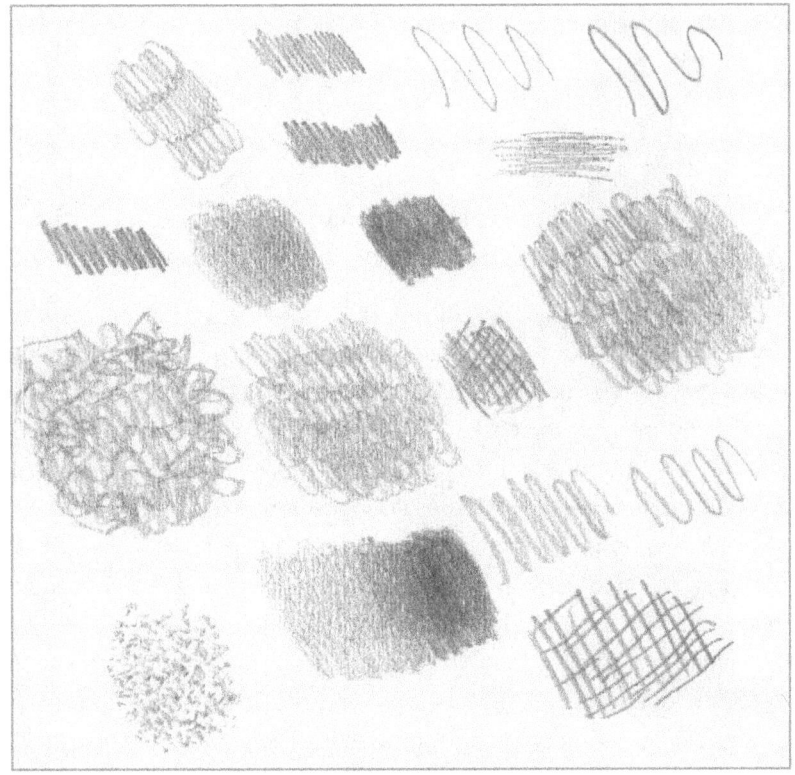

4 See the big picture throughout the drawing stage. Don't sit a few inches away from your drawing whilst it is in progress; you will only gain a segmented view. Mistakes will become invisible and imbalances in the drawing more likely. As mentioned in chapter 1, the, bossy left-brain appreciates things only in its parts and you are allowing this 'knowing' brain to commandeer your drawing. Get up and stand 10 feet away, or at least hold it at arm's length every ten minutes or so during the drawing stage.

5 Turn the drawing upside-down frequently. Yes. Turn it upside-down. In fact, chapter 6 explores upside-down drawing, a great way of allaying the left-brain as the drawing no longer becomes a recognisable object. Turning the picture upside-down will also expose lines that are sloping off or are out of true.

6 View the drawing through a mirror. Taking a small hand mirror to view the drawing through also reboots the brain. It will reveal wonky lines, inaccurate angles and squashed up areas of the drawing. Why not go one step further and view the drawing upside down *and* through a mirror? I often do this if something is troubling me about a drawing or composition and cannot figure out what. If a hand-mirror is not close by, attain a reverse view of the drawing by turning the drawing over and holding it up to the light.

7 Stop looking at the drawing whilst you are drawing. This might sound absurd, but not looking at the subject matter enough during the drawing stage allows memory to sneak into your drawing. What are you drawing whilst you are not observing the subject matter but what you 'know' about it? Knowing is not intuitive and relies upon memory. Memory and knowing, as we have seen, is the domain of the left-brain. Spend at least 50% of your drawing time *looking* at the object in front and asking candid questions about it. I refer to the internal dialogue as mentioned earlier. 'That line is a little higher than that one,' or 'this shape is roughly the same size as the one next to it.' Record what you see and not what you think you see. Do not rely upon memory or what you know about the object.

8 Start with the general and work to the particular. Don't begin the drawing with the intricate veins in a leaf. Get the big shapes down first. Simplify the aspect in front of you into a series of large, abstract shapes. Half-closing the eyes will cut out confusing detail so only the large shapes can be seen. Get the big shapes correct first and then break these down into smaller areas. A jigsaw that begins with the large pieces first, working down to the small. Point 4 on seeing the big picture is an ideal accompaniment to this one.

9 Absence makes the perception grow clearer. Don't work continuously on the drawing if it refuses to work out. Take a break. Get away from the drawing for ten minutes or so and then look at it with fresh eyes. In similar fashion to the methods described in points 5 and 6, the drawing is pushed into the realms of the less familiar. Taking frequent breaks from looking at the drawing will lessen the chances of mistakes remaining hidden.

10 Don't be overcritical. You are learning a new skill. Don't be harsh with your first efforts. Keep your drawings private if you feel the need, but take the view you are practicing a new skill. A learner driver never passes the test within the first week. Work towards improvement, but remember, improvement is not always constant. You will experience lapses and plateaus. Learning to draw is often an organic process.

The Five Principles of Drawing

Learning to draw involves exercising the five main principles of drawing. These are:

1 Edges (these are outlines, lines and contours).

2 Spaces (these are shapes and areas).

3 Relationships (how one shape or mark relates to another regarding size and location).

4 Light and shade (the tonality of the drawing).

5 And the whole (gestalt – how the picture looks in its entirety).

I feel it is vital not to exercise these principles separately, but some (or all) from the start. The following exercises address these principles as they arise. Drawing with these principles in mind will aid accuracy in drawing.

Giving your Left-brain a Hard Kick

You may experience a perceptual discomfort as you go through the exercises in this book if you are a chronic sufferer of picture dyslexia. This is because you are giving your left-brain a good kicking for the first time. It will kick back and make insistences about what you see before you. Old habits die hard and these insistences may win over initially. This may show in your drawing. Don't give up if you are dissatisfied with your first attempts. Drawing truthfully for the first time can be like walking on your hands instead of your feet. The secret is to train your brain to see the world in a new way as shown in this book.

As your drawing skills improve (and they will as you go through the exercises) you may find it less necessary to implement some of the techniques described, although a periodic top-up will keep your bossy left-brain in check. Do not do too much at once. In fact, setting aside twenty minutes a day or so to drawing will prove more beneficial than going full-steam for hours at a time. Take a regular break. If the drawing exercise does not work out, put it away and try again another day.

A final note: All the drawings within this book have been completed freehand – no tracing paper, no enlarger, no rulers. You may notice faint lines indicative of false-starts and adjustments, some rubbed out marks, a minor wobble here and there and small imperfections. This is to be differentiated from drawing errors. My drawing of a Lego brick demonstrates the drawings are not aimed for a draughtsman's finish, and (unless you want to enter this field) neither need yours. Learn to exercise a loose and forgiving approach with your drawing as you learn this new skill. In time, you will find your own means of expression.

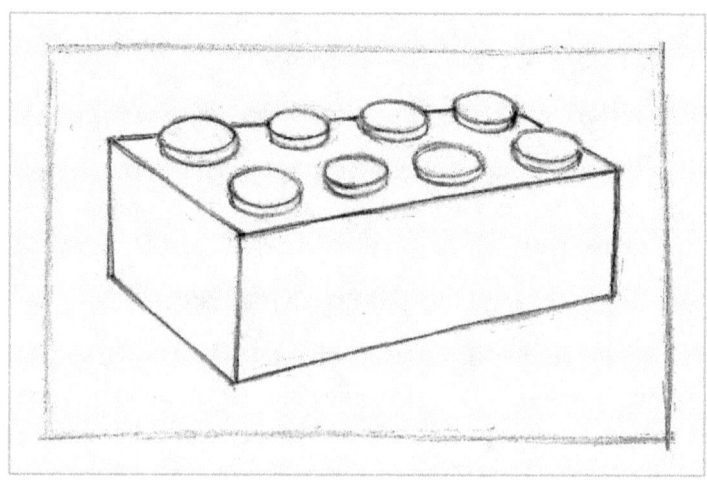

Taking a Line for a Walk

Now have a go at drawing some lines. Taking a line for a walk involves randomly moving the pencil around the paper without it leaving the surface. The pencil, paper or both can be moved around the worktop. Lines must occupy a good portion of all quadrants of the page, creating interesting lines or patterns. The result need not be aesthetically pleasing, but used as a warming up exercise.

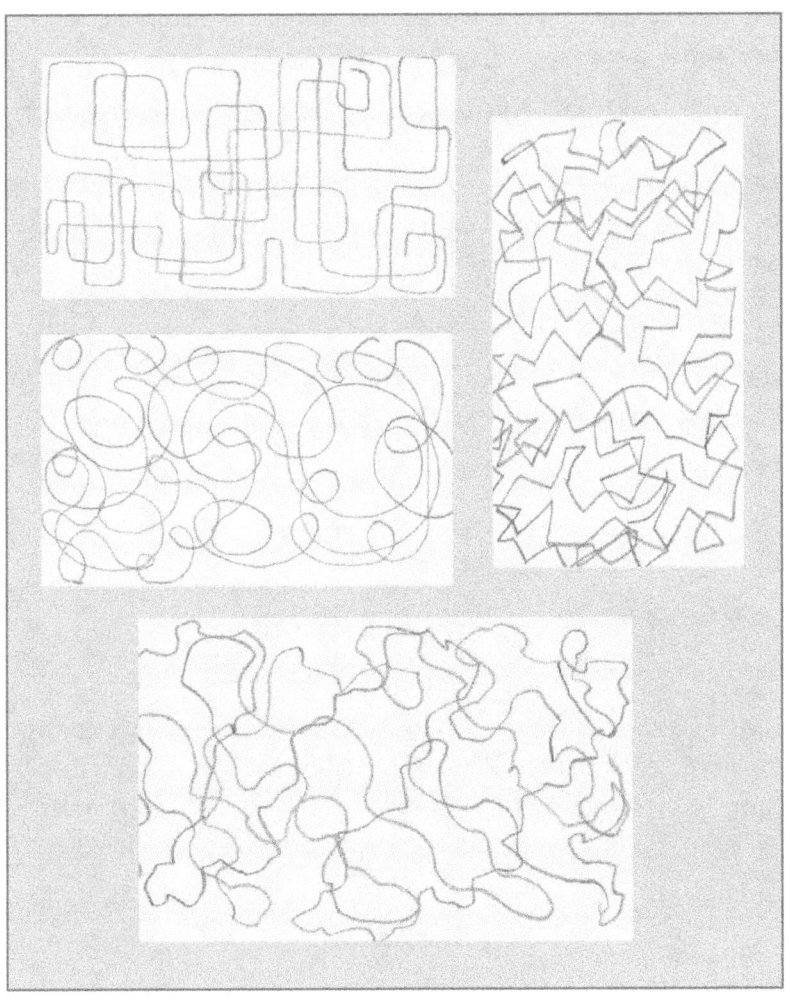

Chapter 3

Chapter 3: Fields of Vision

When I said in the introduction, let's start at the beginning, not with a pair of shoes, I meant what I said. The following exercises require you to draw no such thing but simple lines. The aim is to exercise all your fields of vision, left, right, top and bottom. This has a direct bearing to the test on visual judgment and my research described in chapter 1.

During my teaching, I have noticed that people who struggle to draw suffer from what I consider, 'field-of-vision imbalance.' That is, a higher awareness of one side of an aspect than the other. This will manifest itself when it comes to laying down the lines in a drawing. Here are some indications of this perceptual imbalance:

A drawing that gravitates to one side of the page.

Lines that are supposed to be vertical such as sides of buildings or rigging to ships appears to lean to one side.

A portrait appears squashed at one side.

Lines that are supposed to be horizontal such as window-ledges or tabletops slope off towards the edge of the page.

Circles and ellipses appear sloping and out of true.

The drawing generally appears off-balance, one-sided.

I believe we are all bias a little one way or the other when it comes to drawing. I myself find one side of the drawing easier to work on than the other. To bring this perceptual imbalance back into check, I have devised some drawing exercises aimed to promote awareness of all four fields of vision.

A Perfect Circle

Firstly, try to draw a circle freehand. Don't worry, as few people can actually draw a perfect circle in one stroke. Begin lightly, work around the contour sketchily. A first stroke is likely to yield a circle with a bulge or a flattened side. Rub out and correct. Turn the circle upside down and you may find another deviation, perhaps a flattened edge. Again, rub out and bring this line into accordance. Keep turning the circle this way and that. Gain a reverse view through the mirror. Keep rubbing out to get closer to accuracy. Learn to *look* at the circle and to make accurate visual judgments. It's no good making adjustments to a circle if you remain unaware the circle is fuller on one side than the other.

The point of this exercise is twofold. Firstly it is to prove that no first line will ever be accurate. Drawing entails working towards accuracy. The second is to promote both fields of vision when drawing a symmetrical form. This will also help exercise visual awareness. See the following image to see how a circle can be drawn with increased accuracy in stages.

<u>Perfecting a Circle in Stages</u>

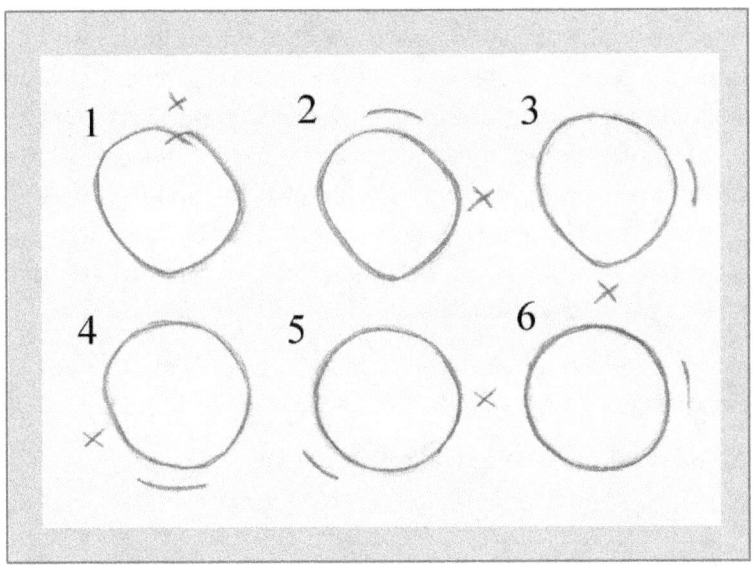

In number **1**, we see an unwanted dimple in the upper arc of the circle. This is rubbed out and evened over.

In number **2**, we see an unwanted lump in the right arc. This is rubbed out and the contour flattened slightly.

In number **3**, we see the lower arc appears distended. This is rubbed out and the curve brought in a little.

In **4**, we can see the lower left arc appears flattened. This is rubbed out and the curve rounded off.

In **5**, a minor adjustment is needed to bring the right side of the circle in balance with the left. This is rubbed out and redrawn so that both sides appear equal.

In **6**, we make progressively smaller adjustments to the circle, turning the drawing this way and that, to decipher deviations in order to correct.

This exercise not only practices hand-coordination, but also the more important visual awareness – the ability to judge if something looks 'right.'

Drawing Symmetry Freehand

The following images show a series of symmetrical compositions beginning with the simplest. I have drawn them freehand, as I would like you to. Do not use a ruler and do not use a compass. Work loosely, take as much time as you wish and use the eraser if required. Don't worry if the lines aren't ruler-straight. Aim for freehand-straight. Use the edge of the paper as a guide when drawing the initial rectangle and then draw your lines in parallel. Like the circle exercise, doing so will practice hand-to-eye coordination as well as visual judgment. You may find one side of the diagram easier to draw than the other.

During these drawing exercises, remember to practice the **A, B and C of drawing** as outlined in the previous chapter, but are abridged here.

The first line will never be accurate. Work towards accuracy.

Start light and work darker.

See the big picture. Hold the drawing at arm's length frequently

Turn the drawing upside down.

View the picture through a mirror.

And whilst copying the drawings, aim for:

Symmetry.

Perpendicular lines.

Equal portion of spaces within each quadrant.

<u>Symmetrical Drawing 1</u>

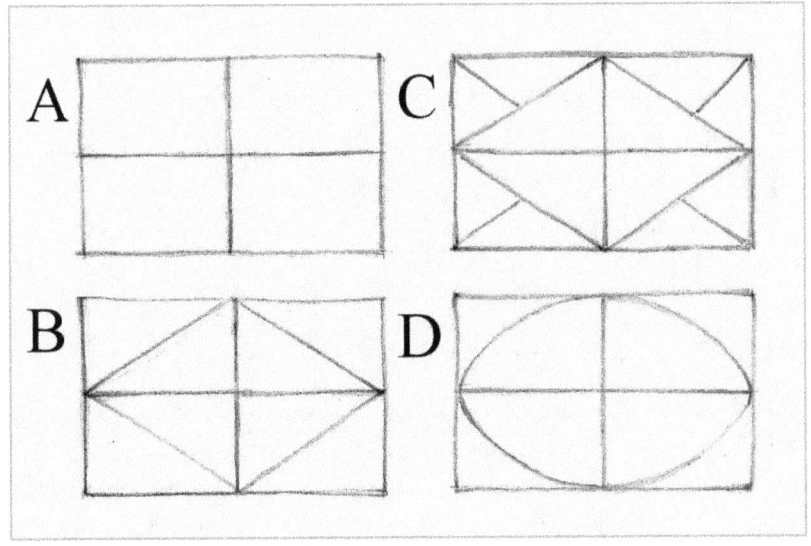

Ask yourself: Are the lines upright/horizontal?

Does each quadrant comprise the same amount of space?

Are there any imbalances between left and right, top and bottom?

Remember to keep looking out for deviations and to keep correcting. Exercise visual judgment throughout.

With more confidence, work larger. This will add challenge to the task. A long straight line is trickier to draw than a short straight line.

Once you have completed the exercise, check accuracy by using a ruler. How perpendicular are the lines in reality? Are they close to true or have your eyes deceived you?

The diagrams below are a little harder as they feature curved lines without straight lines to anchor them to.

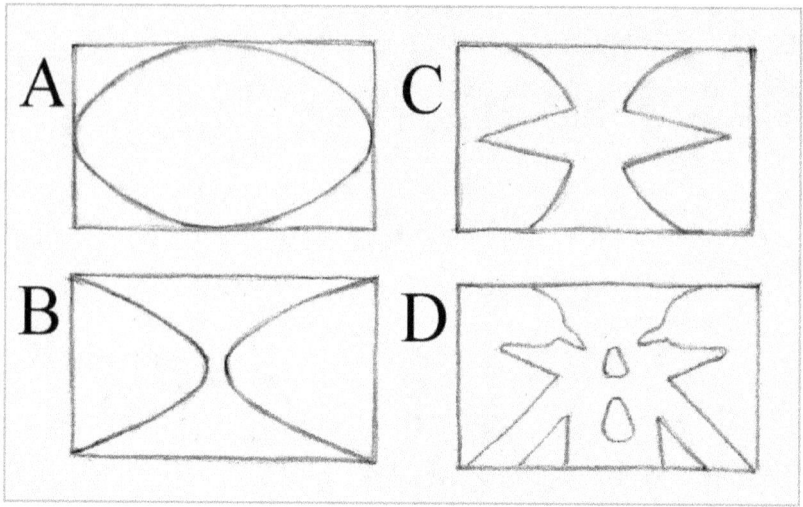

Similarly, check if the centre-point of each image is actually in the centre. Assessing visual accuracy in this way is a good way of checking how accurate your visual perception really is when drawing the symmetrical images. A significant difference between the two will indicate a need to practice symmetrical drawing again another day.

Drawing Symmetrical Objects

Many everyday objects have symmetrical elements, so getting symmetry right will really improve our drawing. Have a go at drawing the following symmetrical objects which consist of a teapot, an eggcup and a vase. Drawing a faint cross in the centre of each may help achieve better symmetry (make sure it is upright and perpendicular). Don't worry if the detail is not accurate, just aim for symmetry in the main body of the object.

If you feel ready, have a go at other objects with symmetrical aspects: coffeepots, scissors, violins, wineglasses, vases, spectacles, cameras and so forth.

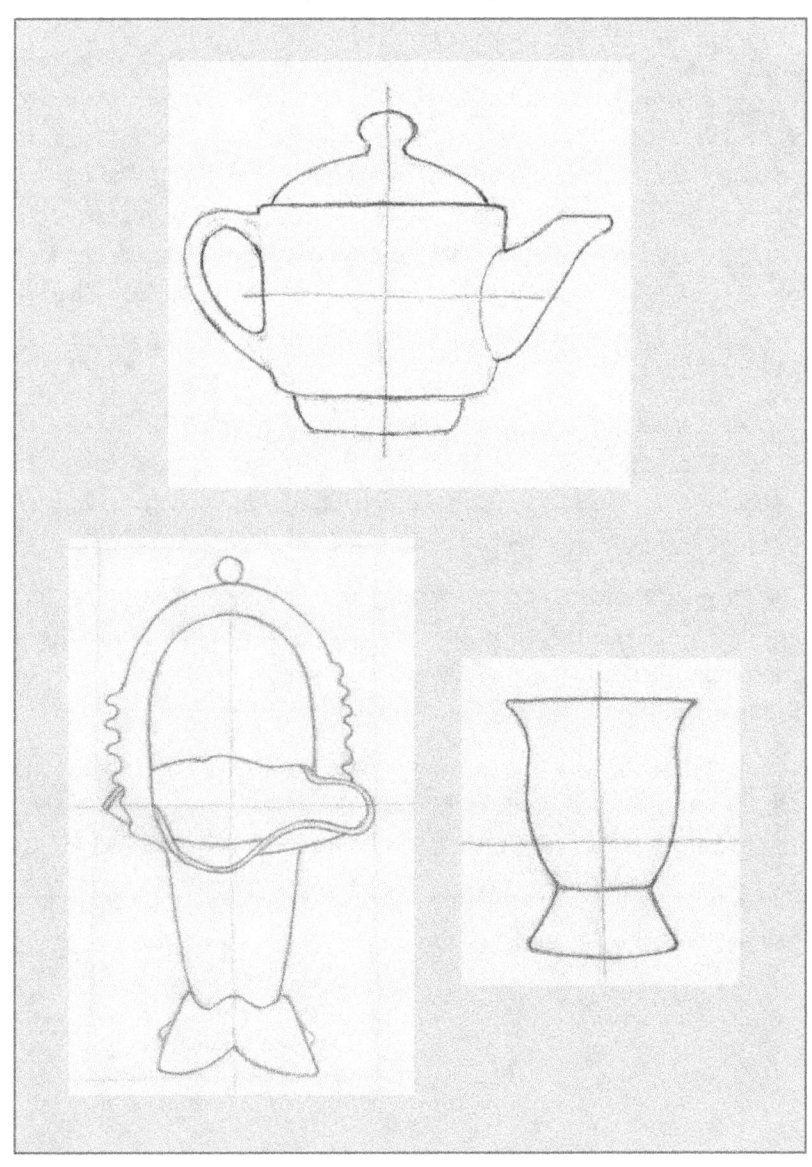

Chapter 4

Abstract Shapes

As mentioned in chapter 1, the left-brain categorises everything around us. Without some sort of categorising system, how would we know what we are talking about, or even be able to communicate? A bird must have defining features that differ from a hippopotamus, otherwise, how would we be able to manage our thoughts? And yet the right-brain makes associations. A cloud *can* look like a cigar; a chair *can* look like a bureau. A painting depicting a pipe could in fact be a carpet that looks like a pipe. It just depends on how you look at it.

Dispelling labels for things is the key to drawing truthfully. This means viewing objects as abstract lines and shapes, not by what they are categorised as. This also means viewing objects as though never seen before or even knowing the names for them.

The following exercises entail evaluating and drawing abstract shapes that resemble nothing in particular. This will exercise the part of the brain that is constantly silenced by the left-brain. There is no chair, bird or hippopotamus to be defined.

Let's begin with a quiz. The following images: The Guitar and The Racing Car comprise linear illustrations with abstract shapes shown on the right. These abstract shapes have been taken from the drawings themselves.

Can you locate the abstract shapes within the drawings? Answers can be found after the two images.

The Guitar

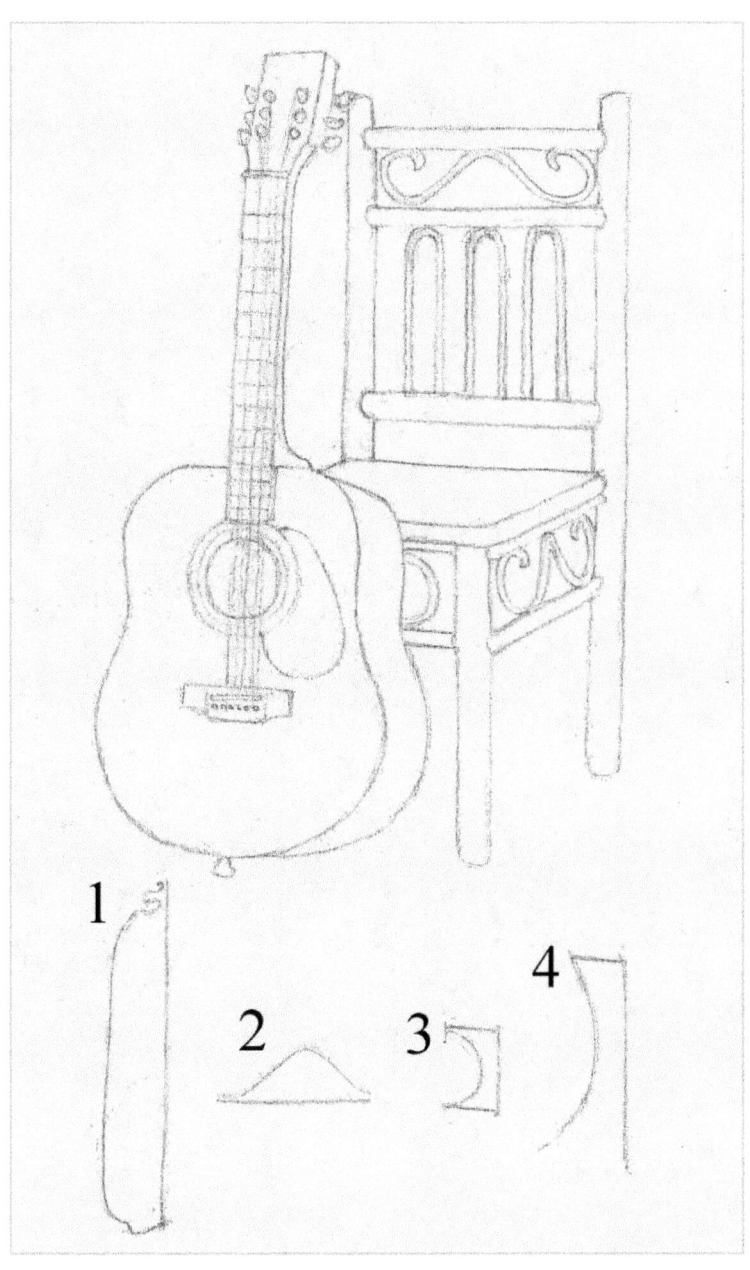

The Racing Car

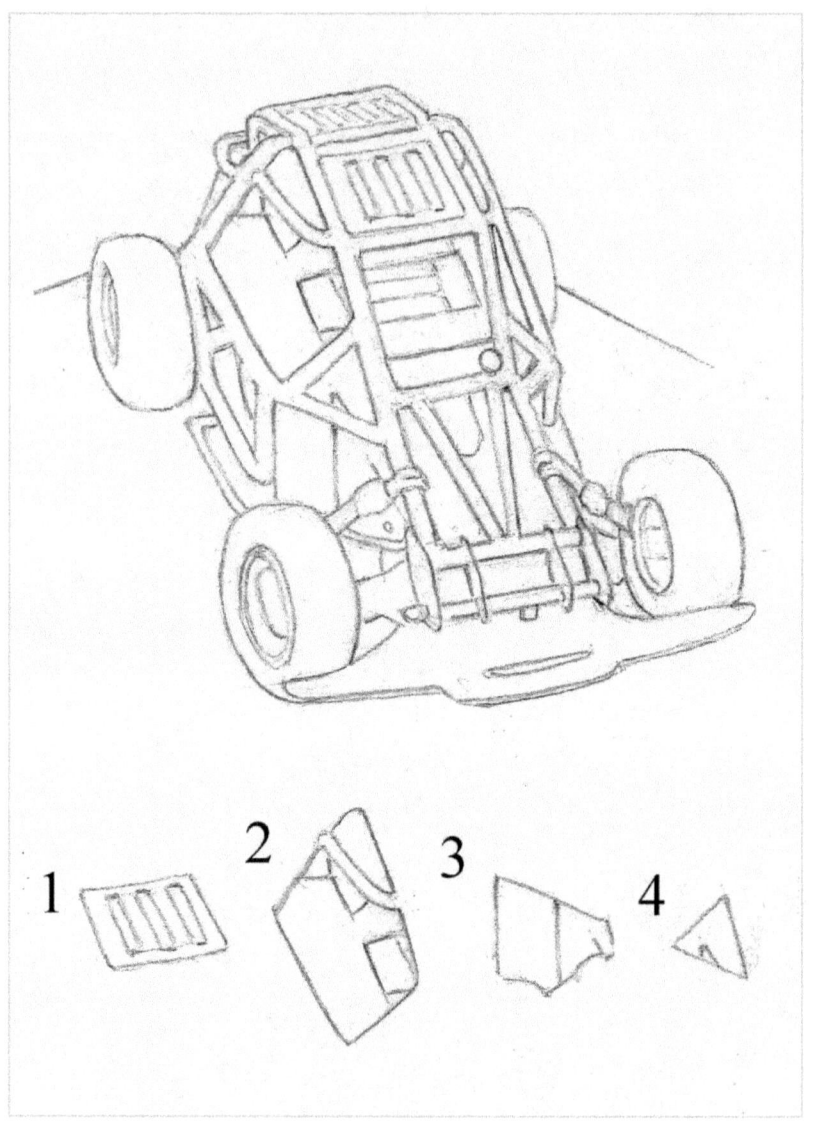

1

2

3

4

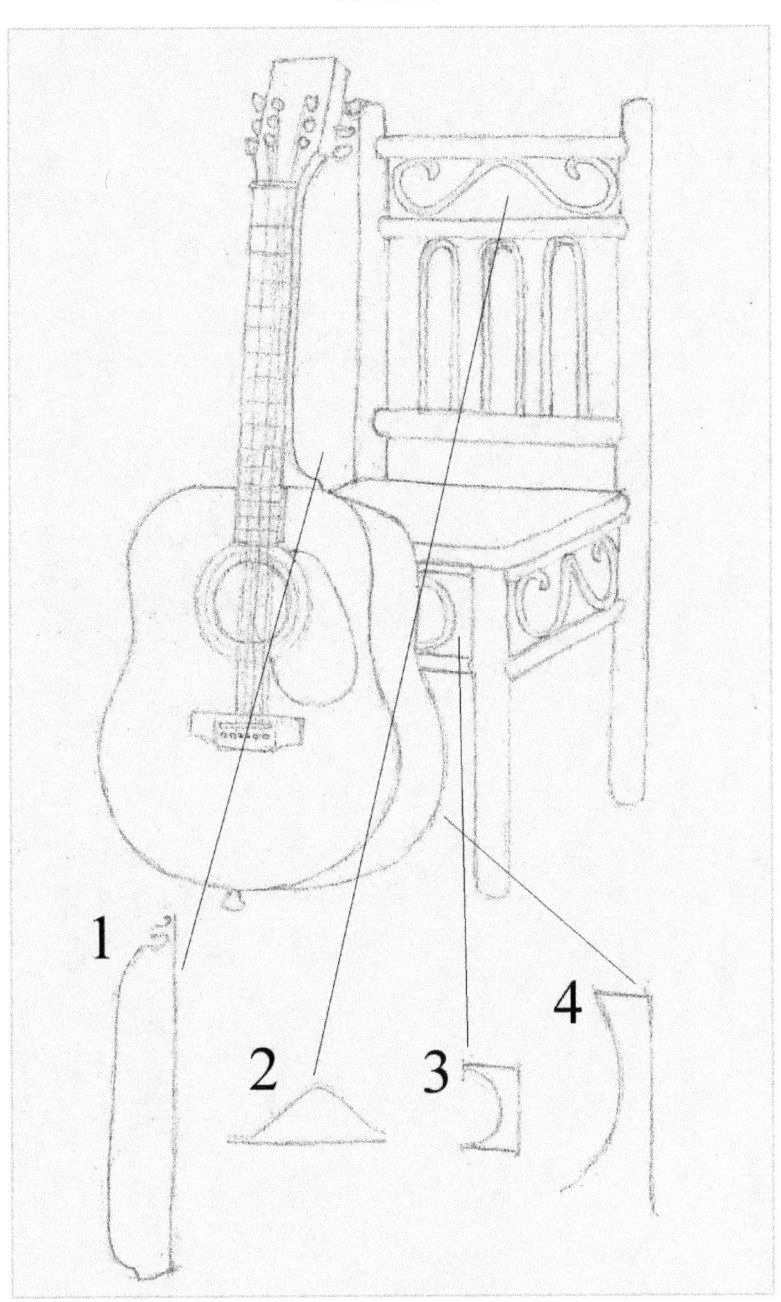

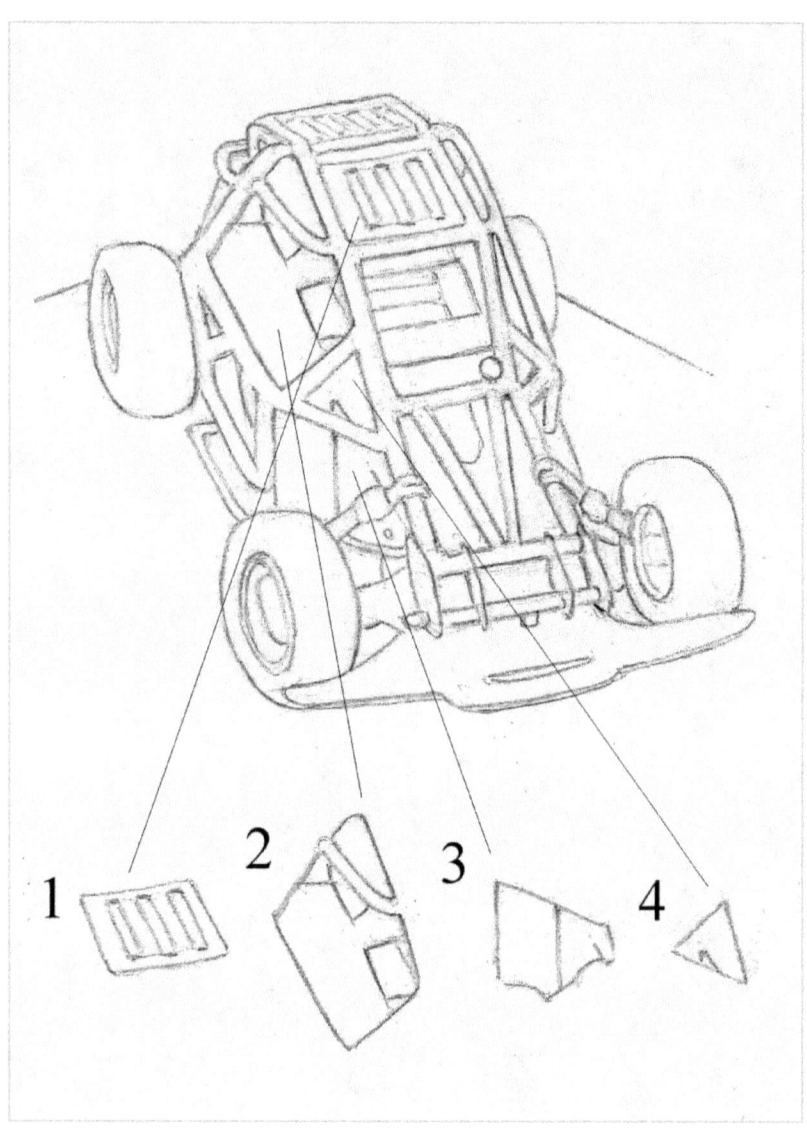

1   2   3   4

This exercise might be a little tricky, but it is excellent for practicing visual observation. A few things are worthy of note:

The abstract shapes can rarely be described. They are often not 'square' or circular' or 'rectangular' in formation, but irregular, nonfigurative.

Sometimes they may resemble something, such as a crescent moon or a trilby or a combination of two objects. When drawing such objects, remember it is the right-brain you are tapping into, the hemisphere that does not deal with words or categories, but pure imagery.

Drawing abstract shapes

Now have a go at copying some abstract shapes. The following images are arranged by challenge.

Images **A** and **B** comprise simple lines that interconnect at various junctions. These junctions will make visually-calculating the lines' contours a little easier as you can see how one line relates with the other.

Image **C** possesses more complex shapes. **D** exercise judgment of how marks relate to one another without lines or marks linking them together. This is a little more difficult to do, as they appear in isolation. Attempt only once you have had a go at the others. Whilst drawing the shapes, ask yourself:

How big is that shape in relation to the other shapes?

In which quadrant does the shape reside? Is it roughly central, to the left, right; on the high side, or further down?

Define each shape's outline, its incline, curve or contour.

I have drawn my own frames for the illustrations but you may use a ruler to draw yours.

Remember to make visual estimates. Look out for hidden inaccuracies. If you feel you are getting 'picture blind,' reboot your brain: take a break, turn the drawing up-side down, view it through a mirror.

Abstract drawing

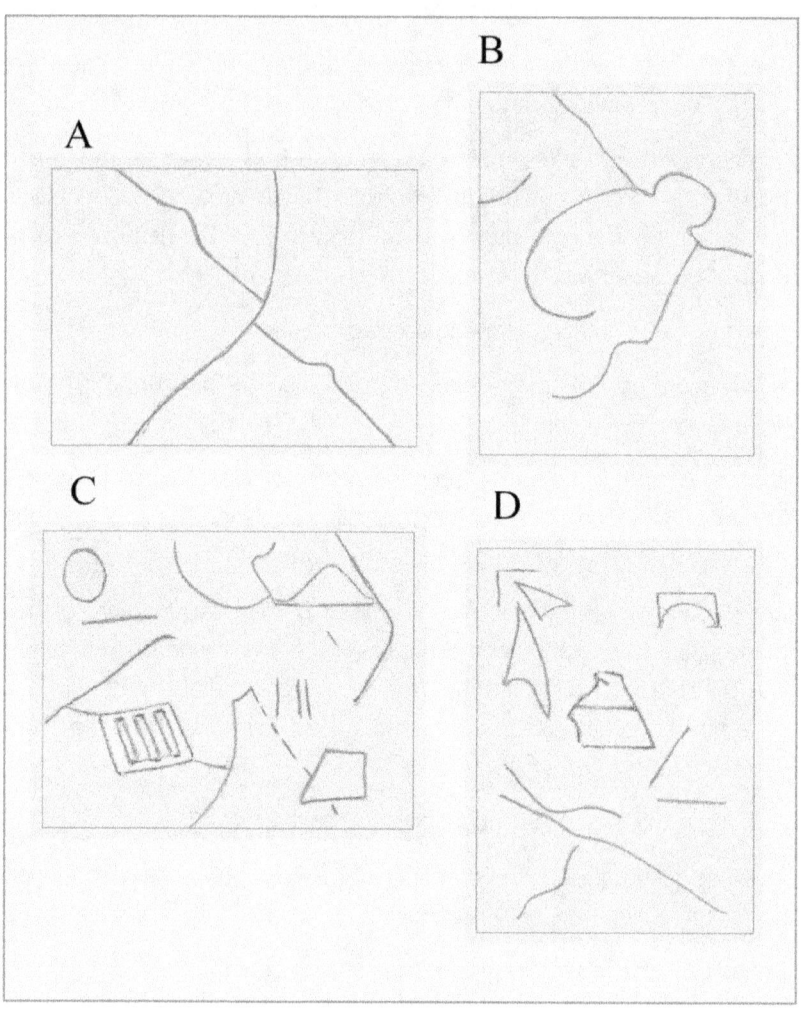

Do you recognise any of the abstract shapes in **C** and **D**? You might find that they can be found within the previous line drawings of the guitar and the racing car.

Image **C** possesses shape 1 of the Racing Car and shape 2 of the Guitar; image **D** possesses shape 3 of the Racing Car and shape 3 of the Guitar.

Chapter 5

A Picture within a Frame

We view the world unabridged, without a lens or viewfinder. In order to see more of the view, all we have to do is turn our head, look up or look down. Our brains piece together the information into a seamless view. All this jumble of information can be tremendously overwhelming when it comes to drawing what is in front of us. Where do we begin? What lies at the edge of the page?

This is why I always think about the extremities of my compositions when I draw. Without this 'frame', there is little to anchor the lines to. It would be trying to draw something, beginning from the centre of a large piece of paper. This is why I would advise beginners to draw a frame before embarking the drawing.

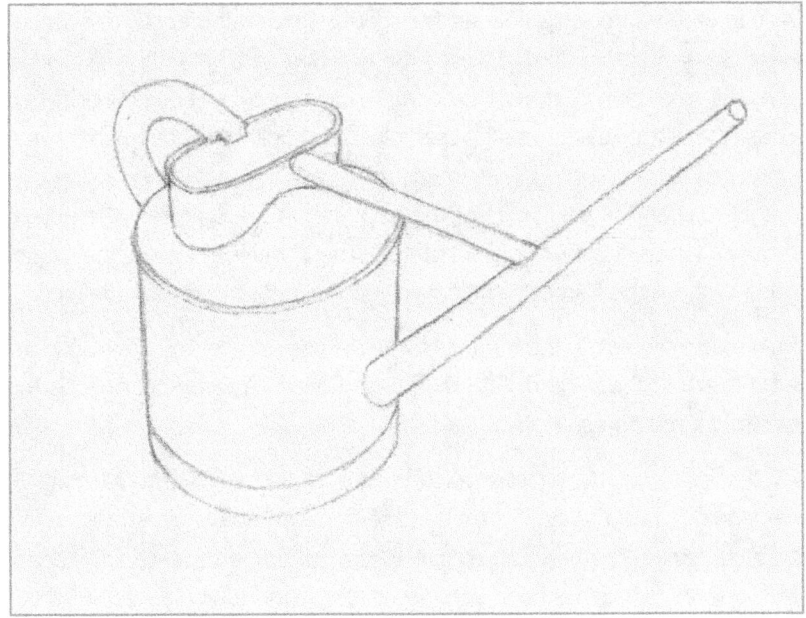

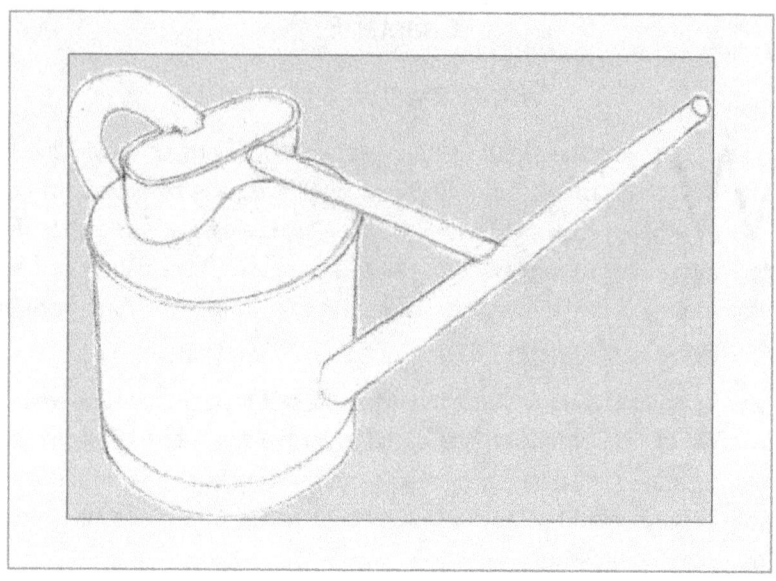

As can be seen from the images, the shape of the watering can in isolation is not so easy to pin down. We see the watering can, but little background shape. The watering can within the frame can more easily be defined when confined within a frame. It resembles a simplified jigsaw where the watering can fits into. This image also shows something known as 'negative space' in the shape of the background areas around the object, most of which are triangular in shape. The positive shape is the object itself. Without this frame, the negative space cannot be so easily defined.

I never use the edge of the paper to define the edge of my drawing or to let the size of the page dictate the proportions of my composition, as the two might not agree.

I will select what I want to draw and then draw my own frame (faintly). Depending upon the subject matter, the frame can be large, small, square or rectangular. You may use a ruler to draw a frame for ease and speed. But drawing lines freehand whenever the opportunity arises will help exercise steadiness of hand and promote visual judgment.

Decide upon what you want to draw and then make a visual evaluation on whether the composition in front is roughly square in its proportions, higher than it is tall or taller than it is high. This does not pertain to the object itself, but how it appears in front of you. A corkscrew might be long in shape, but from a foreshortened view appear short. Don't worry about the drawing fitting neatly into your frame; allow some space around it to give leeway.

Once you have drawn your frame, you can then complete your drawing without fear essential elements will encroach upon the edge of the drawing paper or fall off the edge. You may extend the background into the margin if your wish. When deciding upon the frames for your drawing, here are some options you might try.

The upper image shows the paper in landscape mode, which might feature two sketches. The lower image shows the paper in portrait mode that is to feature a drawing that is rather square in proportions.

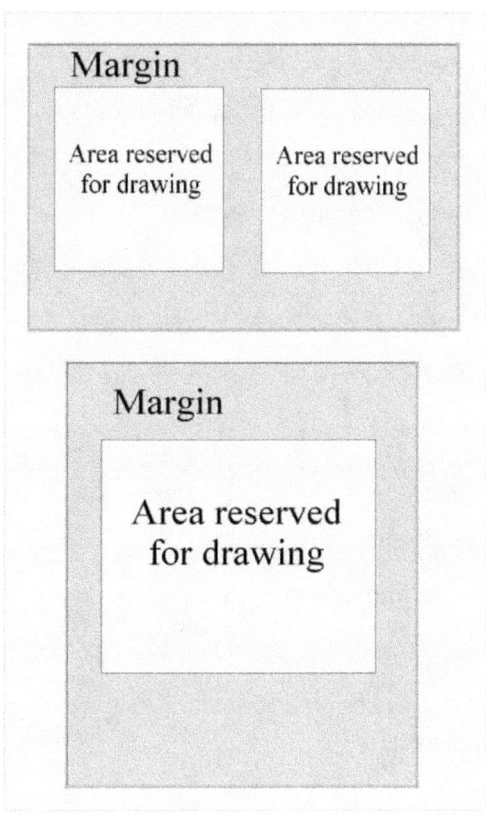

Putting pictures in frames makes drawing more manageable in that:

It edits out unwanted information.

It reveals negative space.

It breaks the drawing down into clear shapes.

The background shape can be equally discerned as the object itself.

The composition can easily be worked out without fear essential elements will wander off the edge of the page.

Chapter 12 contains a section on making and using your own viewfinder, an ideal tool for viewing the scene in front within a frame. The viewfinder can be used to edit out information for drawing and to find compositions. You may use a viewfinder to aid drawing within this chapter.

For the next exercise, faintly draw a frame. Place the objects' outlines within. Pay equal attention to the background shape as to the subject matter itself. You don't need to shade in the background shapes – these have been coloured in to help you see the negative shapes more clearly.

Ensure the background shapes are accurately drawn before tackling the lines within the subject matter itself.

Record the lines in the same fashion as you have done so when rendering the abstract shapes in the previous chapter. Ask yourself:

What are the largest shapes?

What are their sizes in relation to one another?

What are their locations in relation to one another?

How do the smaller shapes compare regarding outlines and locations?

Remember to:

Start faintly.

Turn the image upside down.

View it from afar.

And remember to be equally aware of all quadrants of the image.

In order to heighten awareness of the background shape, you may color it in brightly.

You may begin with the watering can in the previous image. The following images provide further challenges. Guidance for both can be found afterwards.

Negative Shapes

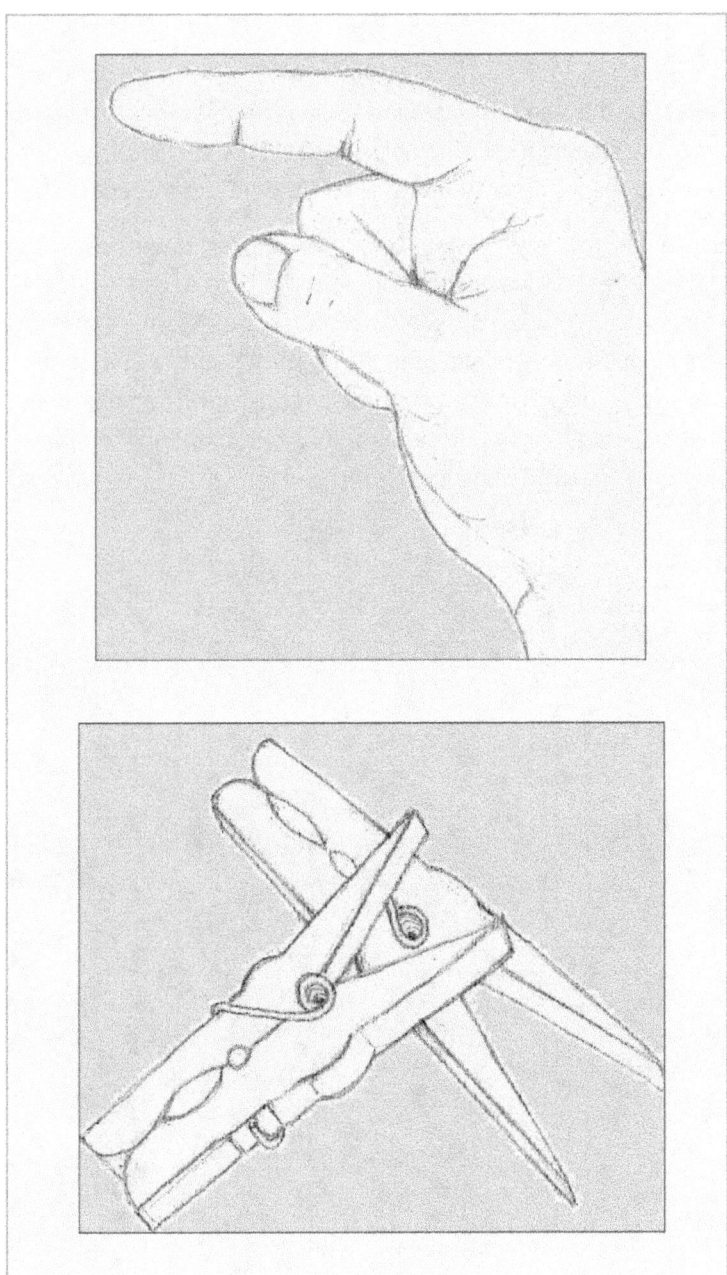

Guidance for the hand: Notice the knobbled triangular shape above the finger. The background shape to the left of the hand features a larger triangle with a projection beneath the pointing finger.

Guidance for the pegs: This image features four triangular shapes in the background. Getting the proportions, relative sizes and locations of these background shapes right will make filling in the subject matter easier.

Guidance for the keys: These keys may appear to possess complex negative shapes until broken down into smaller parts as can be seen within the segmented images on the following page. Segmented image 1 present complex subject matter but the negative shape itself is simple, as it is basically a diagonal line interrupted by a few central extensions. Segmented image 2 comprises a large negative shape that has been cut into by four keys, providing a more simplified view.

Breaking down an image into smaller parts in this way helps to make the drawing more manageable.

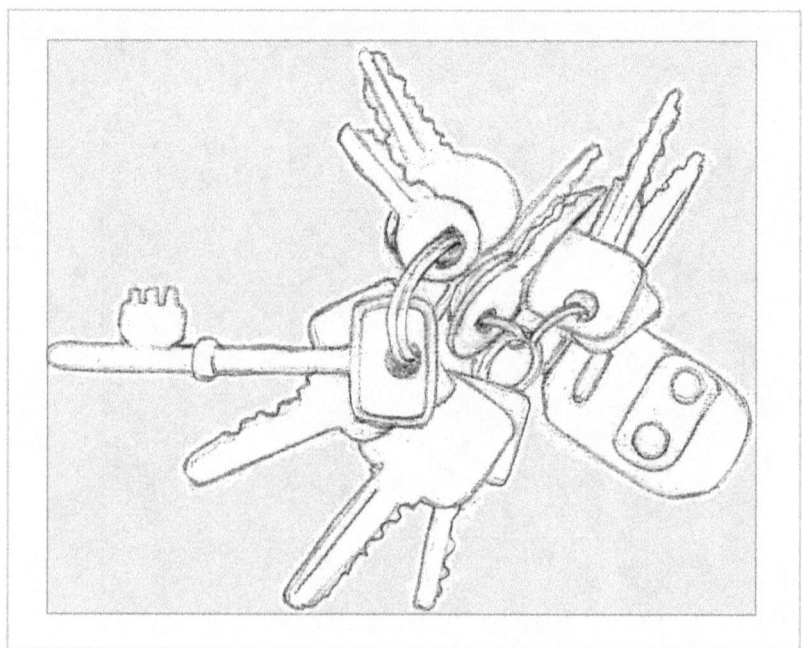

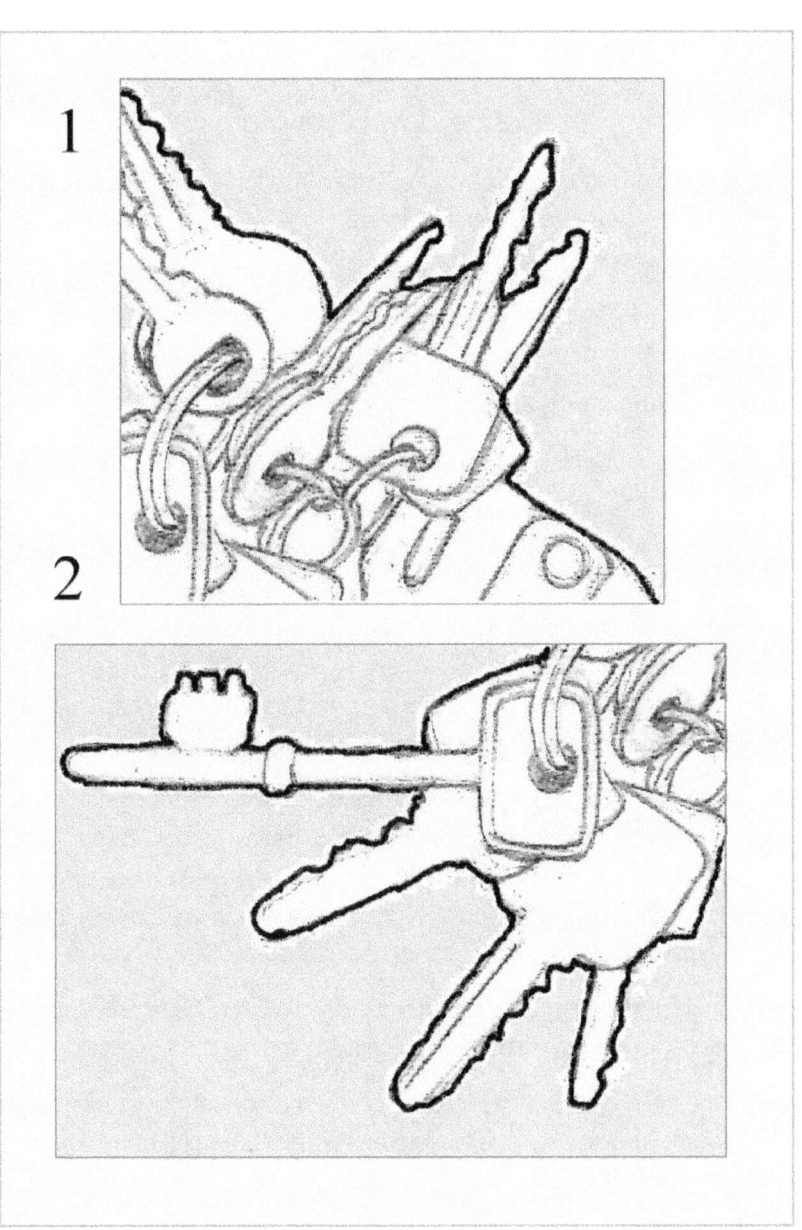

Chapter 6

Upside-down Drawing

Before taking drawing a stage further, a brief recap is necessary, as these new skills will be necessary for the focus of this chapter, upside-down drawing.

Pay equal attention to each quadrant of the page whilst drawing (to promote all fields of vision).

Break down the view in front into abstract shapes.

Place the object within a frame.

Pay equal regard to the negative space as to the positive shapes.

Refer to the A, B and C of drawing.

You may recall that by turning the image upside down, the left-side of the brain is subdued. This is because objects become less recognisable. I will often turn my paintings upside down to gain an abstract view. I will also occasionally turn them onto their side.

The images on the following pages depict subject matter upside down. Each is also placed within a frame to help reveal negative space. The negative space itself has been shaded in to make them more apparent during the exercise. Again, you don't have to shade them in unless it helps with the drawing.

Have a go at drawing the object from this view. Don't be tempted to turn the pictures the right way up until you have completed the drawings.

Tip: draw the negative shapes that lie on each corner of the image first, as they are the largest. The one located on the 'bottom right' of the image is almost a perfect triangle.

Your First Upside-down Drawing

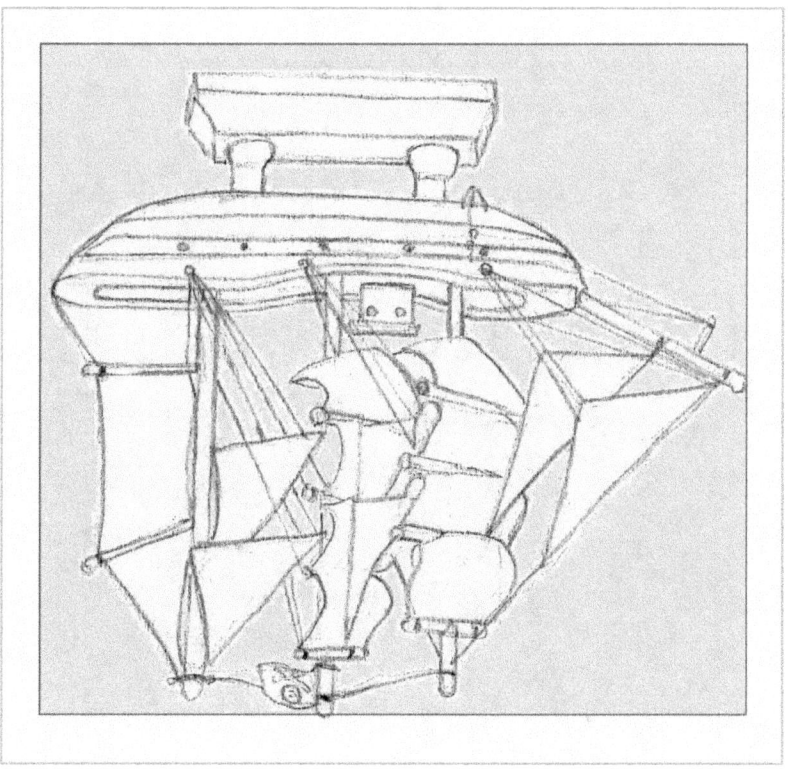

The great thing about this exercise is that you can select any photograph or image and turn it upside-down for drawing. An odd thing begins to happen after exercising upside-down drawing for a while is that you begin to find you can override the left-side of the brain even when the aspect is the right way up – handy if you want to draw from life, as the world cannot be turned upside-down and you cannot always stand on your head.

You may have gathered that this upside-down image features the starting point of your journey into drawing. Take out your earlier version and compare. You should see an improvement.

Have a go at the others. Some comprise complex abstract shapes. Begin by drawing a faint frame that roughly matches the proportions of the subject matter. Sketch in the largest areas first, working down to the smallest. Take note of the background negative shapes as you go along.

<u>Upside Down Drawing 2</u>

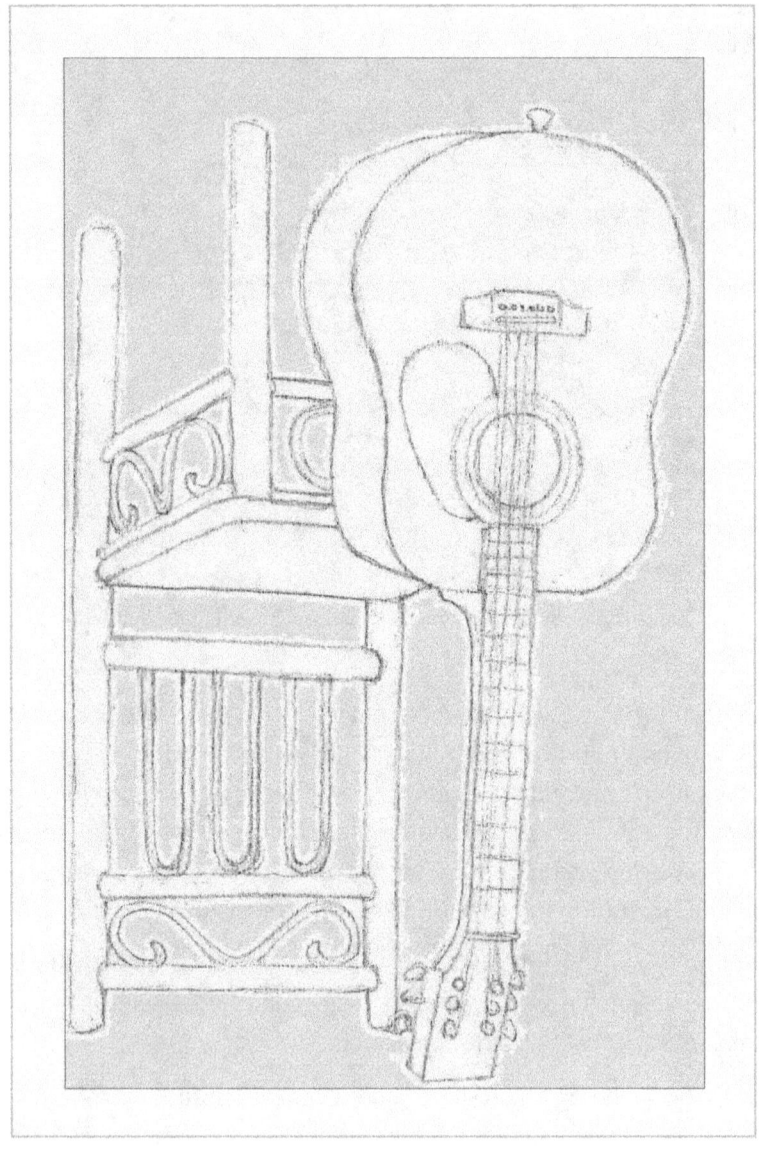

Guidance for no. 2: Notice the large and smaller long shapes on either side of the guitar's fret-board and a sort of inverted F-shape around the foot of the chair. Ensure these shapes are accurately drawn before illustrating the smaller elements. Notice there are seven segments of background-space peeking through the vertical bars of the chair. Get each roughly the same in size before elaborating on the whorls. Practice symmetrical drawing when working on the guitar. Make sure the perpendicular lines of the chair are true to vertical.

<u>Upside Down Drawing 3</u>

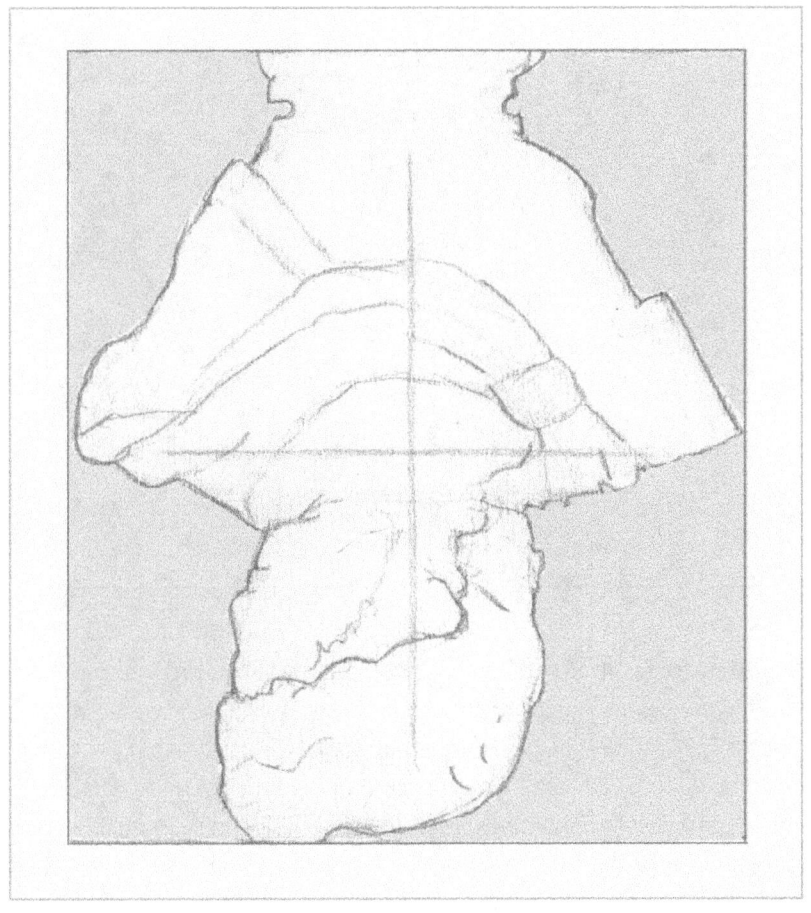

Guidance for no. 3: Two of the negative shapes are almost a mirror-image of one another at the base of the statue. Symmetrical drawing is required here. The other two negative shapes at the head of the statue are roughly square/rectangular. Elaborate upon the contours only once the sizes and locations of each of these negative shapes have been worked out.

<u>Upside Down Drawing 4</u>

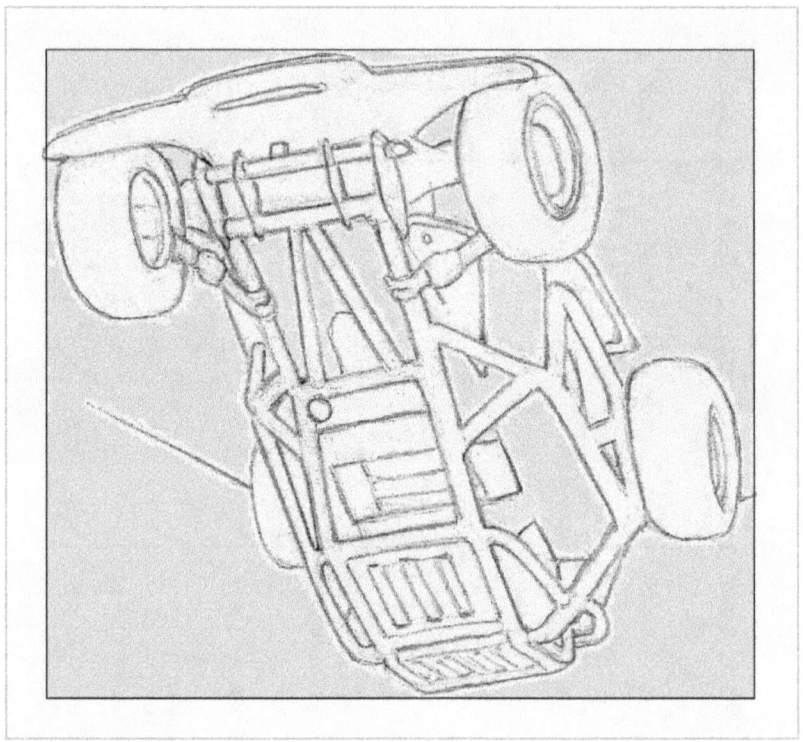

Guidance for no. 4: Notice how the largest areas of background space around the car are roughly triangular in shape. Work into these basic shapes to illustrate the wheels. Take care to get the oval shapes right. The main body of the car can be seen to comprise a series of grids, each interconnecting with the other via rectangles and triangles. Remember to compare how one shape relates to the other, regarding shape, locality and size, working from the largest. This image is not easy; take your time. If you get it right, praise is due.

Chapter 7

Objects in Foreshortening

D rawing long objects in foreshortened view sets up the classic dilemma between the two hemispheres of the brain. The object is long, and yet it does not appear so.

People of low drawing ability frequently insist upon illustrating a side-edge of an object within their drawings to demonstrate that the object is 'long', regardless of whether this edge can be seen or not. This left-brained insistence causes wonky chair legs, skewed scissors and bent-looking corkscrews in drawing.

An object in foreshortened view is not a comfortable sight for the left-brain to process because of the contradiction with what it knows. How can a hairbrush resemble a starfish? (See following image). As can be seen, a hairbrush can take on different proportions in various stages of foreshortening.

Try drawing your hand with pointed finger in two views: the first with the finger pointing to the side; the second with the finger pointing straight at you. This second drawing should be trickier to do than the first. Close one eye during the task to eliminate the parallax view. If you prefer, you may copy my version, which can be found after the following images.

Try other long objects: clothes-pegs, scissors, tin openers, wooden spoons, guitars, hair straighteners, teapot-spouts and cutlery. Imagine they are not what they are or that they are long, but mere abstract shapes. Don't worry if the drawing ends up not resembling the object at all. Drawing a recognisable object is not the aim, but simply to draw what you see.

Try other odd angles too. The underside of a teapot may not look recognisable as a drawing. The following images comprise objects showing various degrees of foreshortening.

Hairbrush

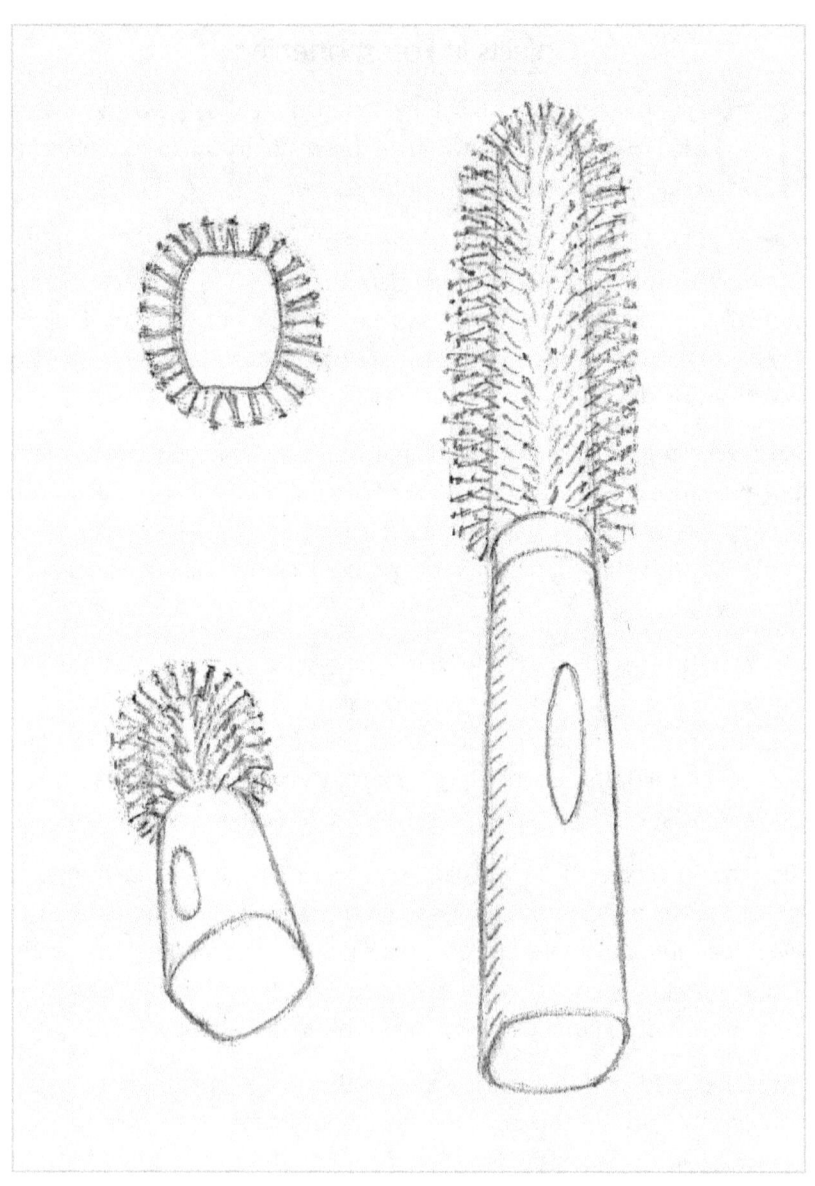

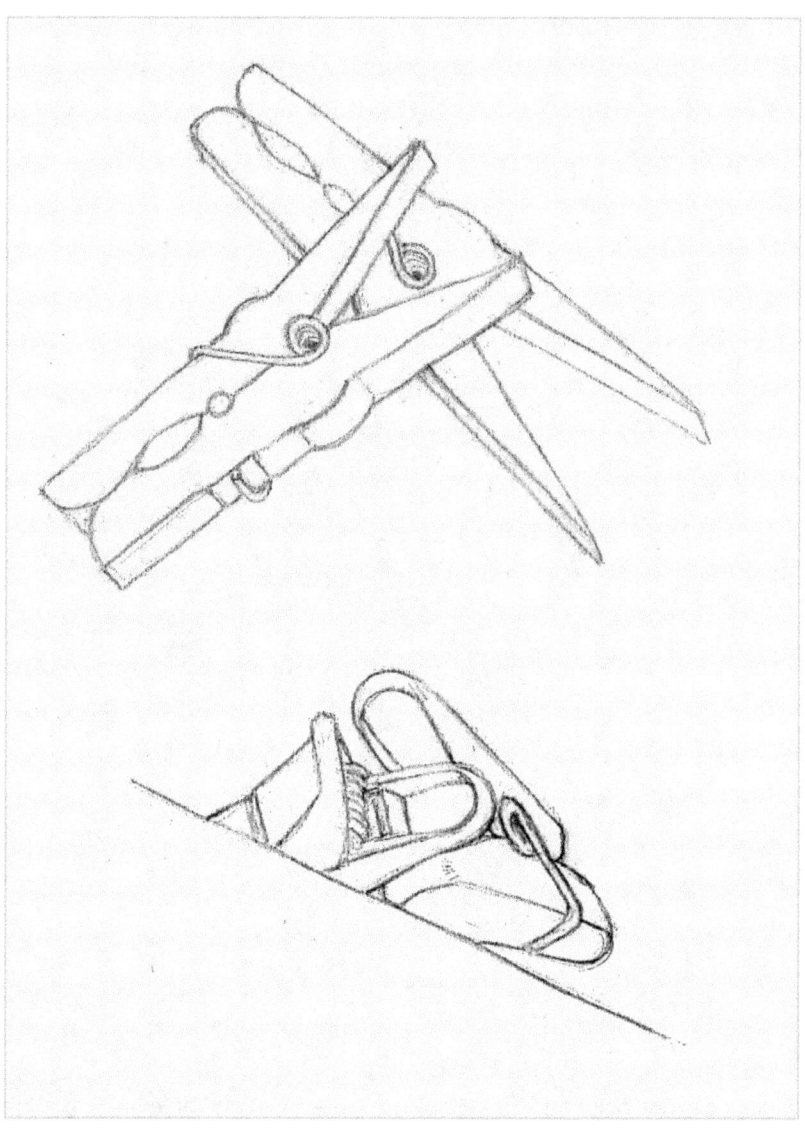

Guidance: Notice how the leading edges of the pegs on the bottom image appear to converge at a steep angle as they recede from the viewer. The drawing above shows how these edges appear to run almost parallel. This is due to the rules of perspectives, covered in chapter 12.

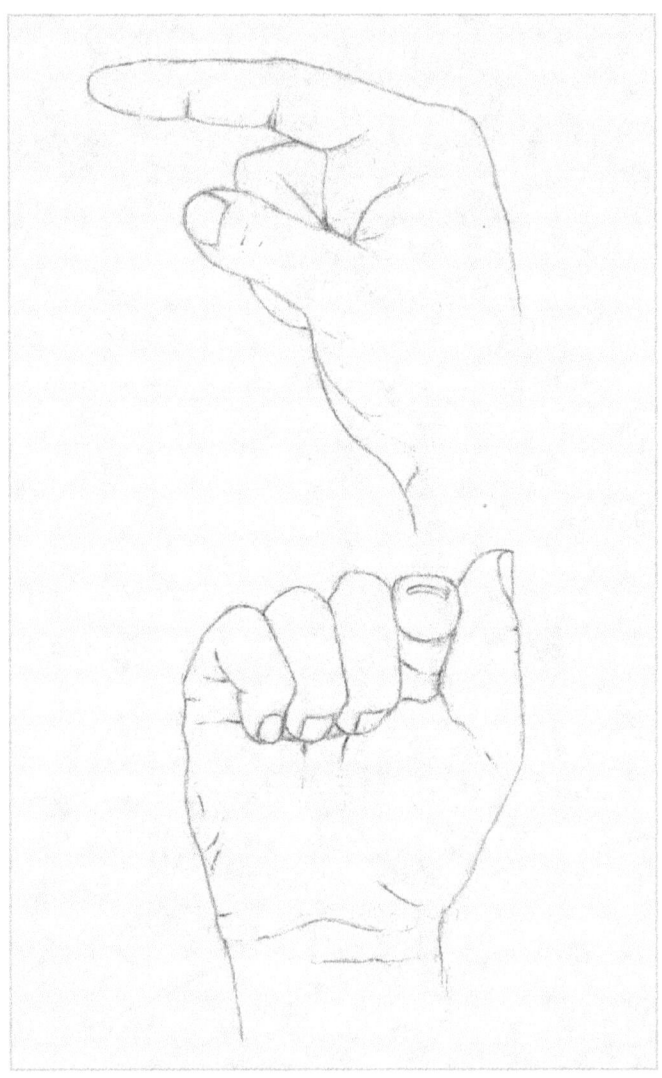

Guidance: The pointing finger does not have a decipherable leading edge to be illustrated, but appears to be a circular shape. Try not to illustrate the length of the finger. Close one eye if drawing your own hand to eliminate the parallax view. Remember to observe how the foreshortened finger relates to the rest of the hand.

Chapter 8

The Weight of Marks

S o far, we have explored symmetrical drawing to raise awareness of both fields of vision in order the tackle lopsided drawing. We have also looked into drawing abstract shapes in order to make visual estimations without interference from the left-brain. We have looked at negative space and upside-down drawing, all whilst practicing the A, B and C of drawing.

This chapter takes a step further: into the weight of line. As we can see, not everything in the world is presented to us as a liner aspect with equal thickness and 'weight.' There is a big difference between a soupcon of subtle lines that comprise a portrait and dynamically rigid lines that make up a metropolis. We are entering the realms of tone. But let's lead into tone via line. In the following exercise, you are to measure not only the gradient of line, but also its weight. Ask yourself:

How thick is the line? Is the line hair-thin or like thick wire? Is it somewhere in between?

Is the outline of the line constant in thickness or does it vary along the way?

What is its tone? Is the line light, dark or a gradient between?

Does the tone of the line vary along the way? Does it get darker, paler, or oscillate?

How defined are the edges of the line? Are the edges harsh or soft? Does this vary?

An aspect of shading will be required for the soft areas and which will be explored more fully in the next chapter.

Remember to check how one mark relates to the other

Practice the A, B and C of drawing.

Turn the image upside down.

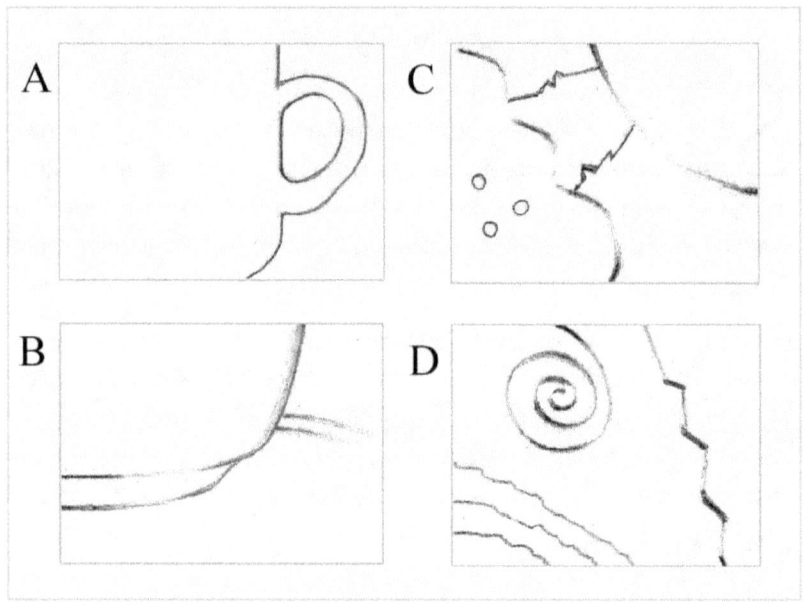

Guidance

A comprises lines of equal 'weight', which requires consistent pressure on the pencil throughout the drawing. Work lightly at first, and then work darker, retaining this evenness in line.

B exhibits a soft edge to the inner edge of the central line. Apply light shading on this side to soften it out. The lines that lead towards the edge of the picture also fade out softly. Gradually apply less pressure on the pencil within these areas.

C exhibits varying degrees of light and dark along the swirly lines. Gradually exert a little more pressure as you work darker around these areas. Notice how the small circles do not alter in tone.

D exhibits varying contours of line, some jagged, others swirly. The zigzag exhibits alternating pale and dark lines which shift abruptly. The 'spiral' also exhibits alternating dark and pale lines but are more gradual in nature.

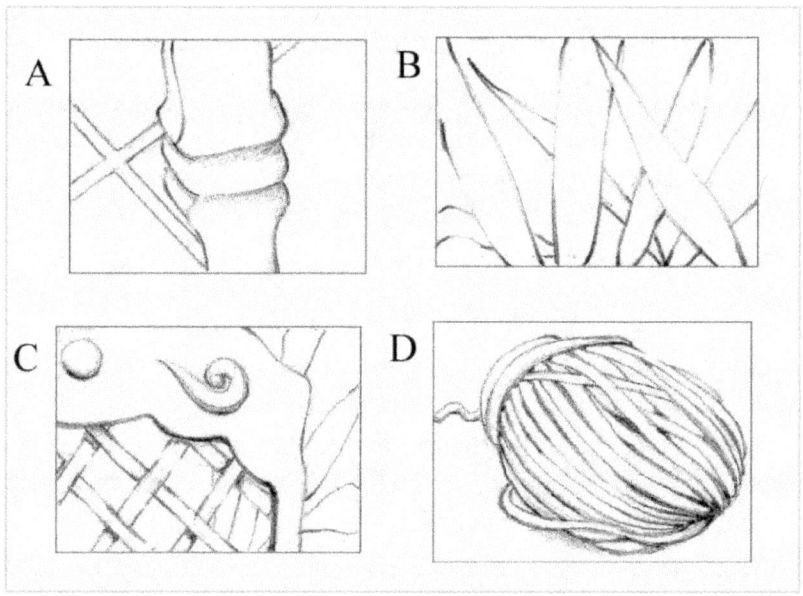

Guidance

A shows a combination of regimented lines and soft edges on the same scene. A little shading is required around the 'table leg' to suggest contours, but not elsewhere.

B shows darker lines at the top and bottom of the 'leaves' and paler lines in the middle. A smooth gradation is required between both tones.

C shows how the weight of lines wavers throughout the weave pattern. A little soft shading is needed to suggest shadow where the 'weave' appears to undulate behind others.

D illustrates varying thickness of line on the ball of string, some of which are wider than others. Most of the lines are diagonal in nature except for a few stray strands at the top. Minimal shading is required.

More advanced exercises on this theme can be found within chapter 11, tackling subject matter possessing subtle lines and shading.

Chapter 9

Light and Shadow

Technique is nothing without accuracy which is why shading is explored after line within this book. But when things go right, shading can really add expression and describe form. We have touched upon shading in the previous chapter, the weight of marks. To really begin shading take note of the following tips into shading.

The A, B and C of Shading

1 As with linear drawing, begin light and *then* work darker. Work over the drawing simultaneously, not in parts, adding the progressively darker shading as you go along. Darken areas in stages, working over the drawing in layers like a painting. Finish with the darkest shading, leaving the palest areas relatively untouched.

2 Don't hold the pencil ninety degrees to the drawing paper or unwanted lines will result. Skid the edge of the nib against the page to create soft marks. Keep rotating the pencil if sharp lines occur, to retain this soft edge. Wear down harsh ridges by scribbling the edge of the nib onto scrap paper before continuing.

3 Try not to shade in horizontal or vertical strokes or this will bring a regimented feel to your drawing. Work the pencil in angular strokes or according to the subject matter's contour. If a smooth, airbrushed effect is desired, work the pencil in small circular motions as shown in 'the orb' in chapter 10. For striations on an onion, work the pencil in the direction of the patterns.

4 For an area of uniform shadow, apply pressure evenly. Work the pencil in roughly the same direction but with the aim of working over lines and unwanted marks to override them. Keep working over the area in layers as described in step 1.

5 For smooth gradations in tone, work the pencil in small circular strokes, overriding sudden tonal increments for smooth gradations. Keep working over the area, adding progressively darker tones to selected areas. Take care not to go too dark if this is not the aim.

6 As with linear drawing, always get an overall view of the tonal study or tones will be hard to judge. Stand back from the drawing and half-close the eyes to gain some distance from the drawing and the image depicted. Observe how tones relate with one another. How much darker is that area than the other? Is it half as dark again?

Sitting too close to the drawing will often give a misleading impression of how dark a tone it. From afar, it may not appear so dark.

The images below illustrates how tonal areas viewed close up can only be appreciated in its parts, not how it relates with the whole subject matter. As can be seen, viewing an image from afar makes it possible to see how tones relate to one another. This helps make the picture make sense during the drawing.

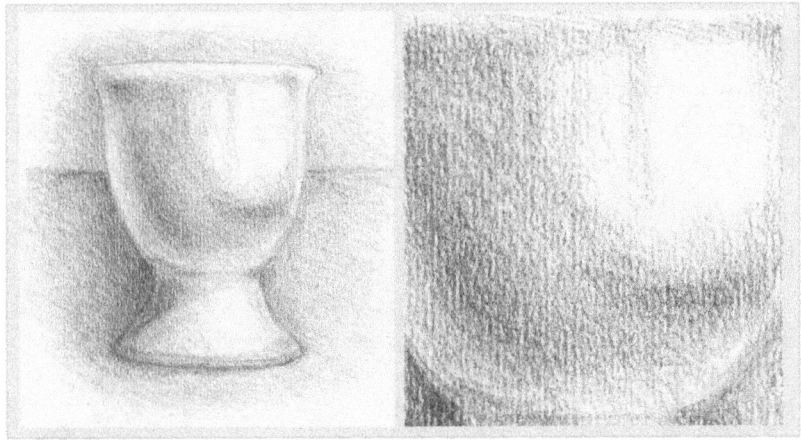

The following exercises feature images that enable the practice of shading in levels of challenge. Follow the guidance as best you can to enhance your drawings in the latter part of this chapter and if you wish to progress to chapter 11.

Tonal Values

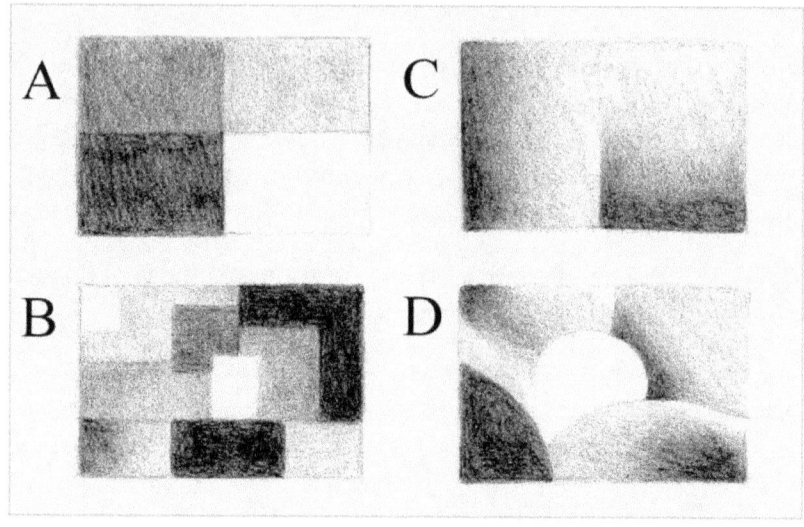

Guidance

A comprises four quadrants of flat tones. Use the soft edge of the pencil to create even shading, working over each area via even strokes. Work over in stages, overriding unwanted marks. Don't go too dark initially or you will have little leeway to go darker for the other squares.

B is a little more complex as we see more shapes, but again, features flat tones. Look for shapes similar in tone, such as the shapes on either side of the central white square. Keep comparing how one tone relates to another. Watch out for squares that possess a shift in tone.

C comprises two tonal areas grading out. Apply progressively less pressure via the pencil when working towards a paler shade. Again, work the area in layers, not in one go to achieve smooth gradations.

D requires sensitive observation of tones, such as the fuzzy crescent shape at the bottom of the image and the light-bulb shape in the centre. Take note not all shapes possess a shift in tone.

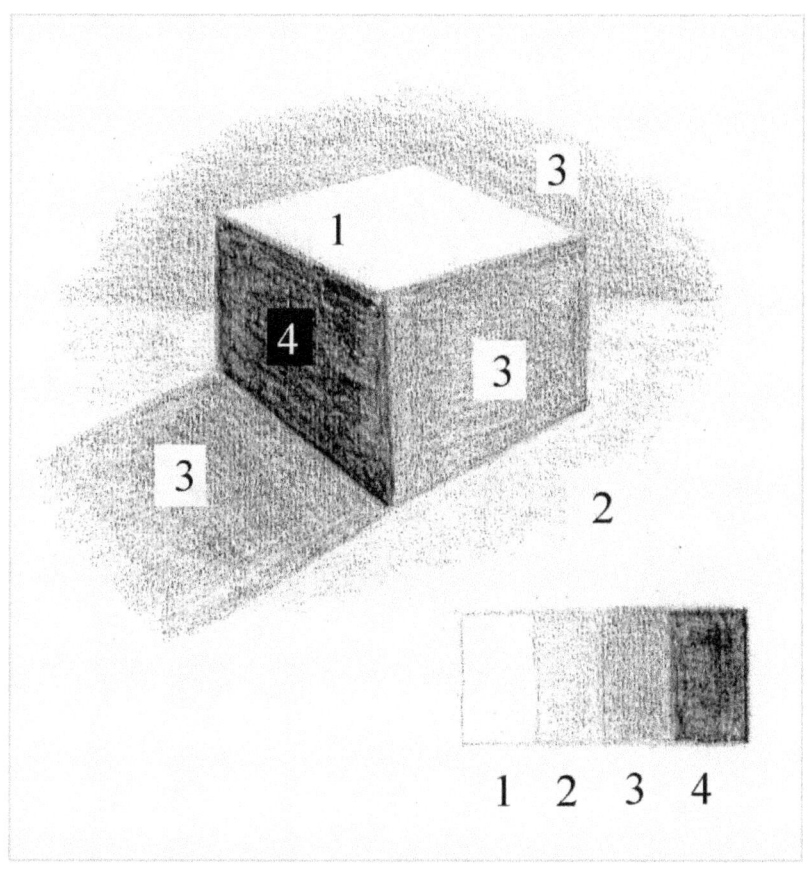

Guidance: This cube comprises a mere 4 tonal values. (If you have problems with drawing cubes, chapter 12 offers guidance on drawing regular shapes.) This illustration comprises flat tonal areas, the key to which can be seen on the bottom right.

Try to apply each tone evenly as you have done so within **A** and **B** of the previous exercise. Remember to make a visual judgment of how paler or darker one tone is compared with the other.

<u>Cube 2</u>

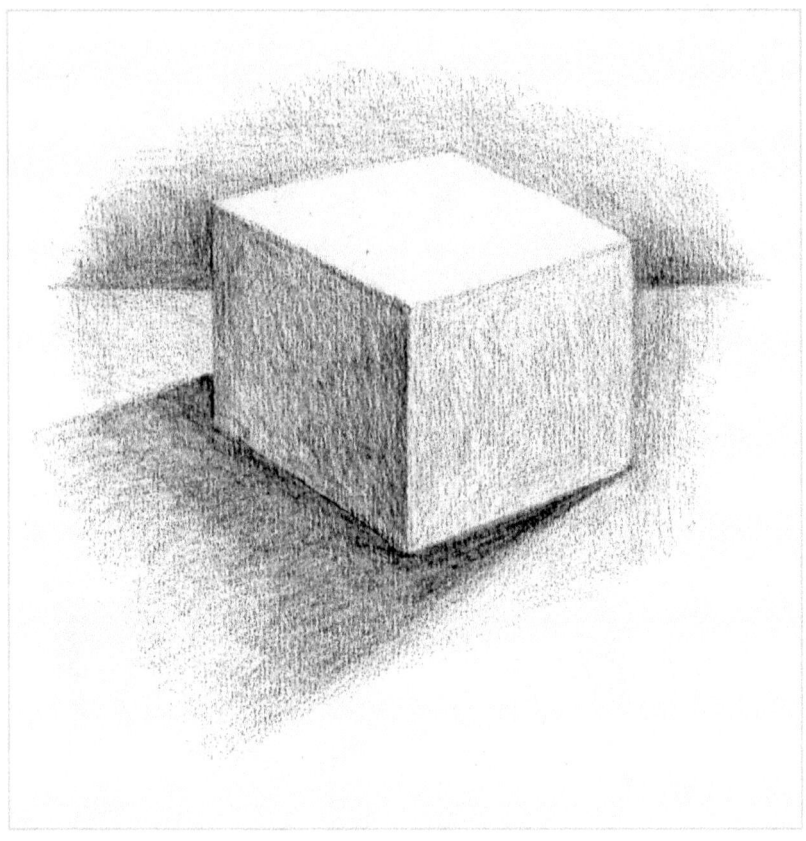

Guidance: Now draw the cube again, but this time, elaborate upon each tonal area as shown, introducing some gradation. Work the pencil in faint crisscrosses to introduce a little expression into your shading. Fade out towards the edges of the drawing to get a real feel of how much pressure is required on the pencil to obtain a variety of tones.

Now have a go at shading the following objects which comprise symmetrical elements and which possess a mere four to five tonal values. Each drawing will require further elaboration within each area as well as sensitive gradations. Practice symmetrical drawing as shown earlier in this book prior to shading.

Teapot

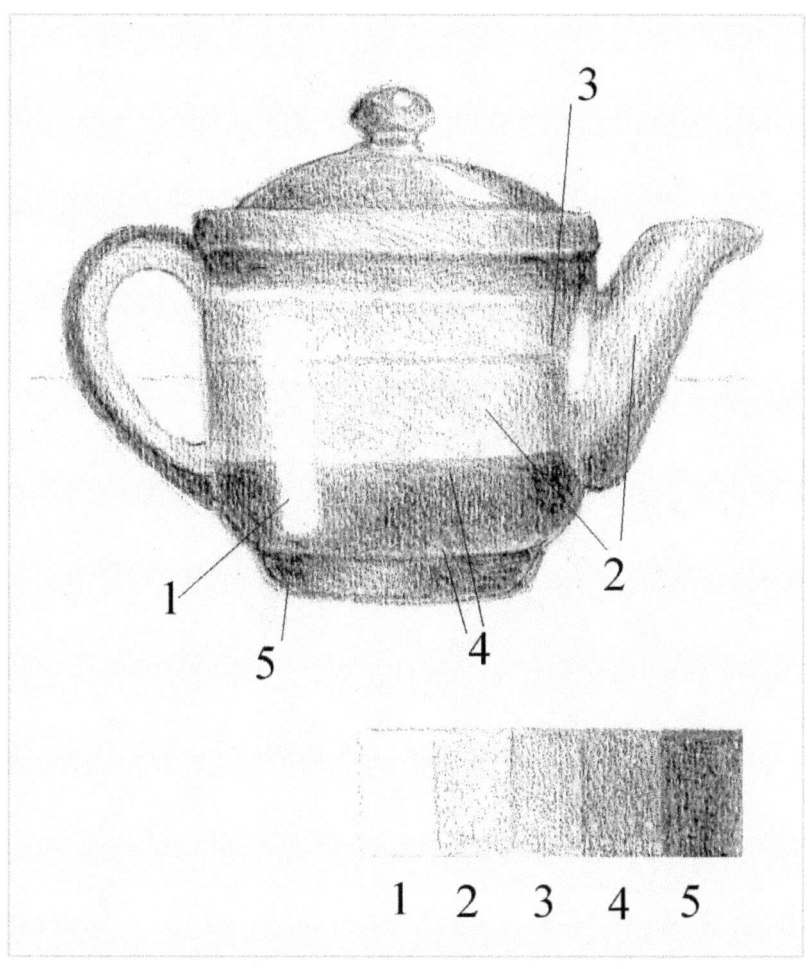

Guidance: draw the teapot using the methods shown in chapter 3 on drawing symmetrical objects, not forgetting the A, B and C of drawing. Draw a faint central cross and ensure each side of the teapot is symmetrical. In similar fashion to the drawing of Cube 2, shade in some areas flatly, but elaborate on other tonal areas. As a rough guide, you will find a key to tones on the bottom right. Apply progressively more pressure upon the pencil as you work darker and be careful not to go over the highlights.

<u>Eggcup</u>

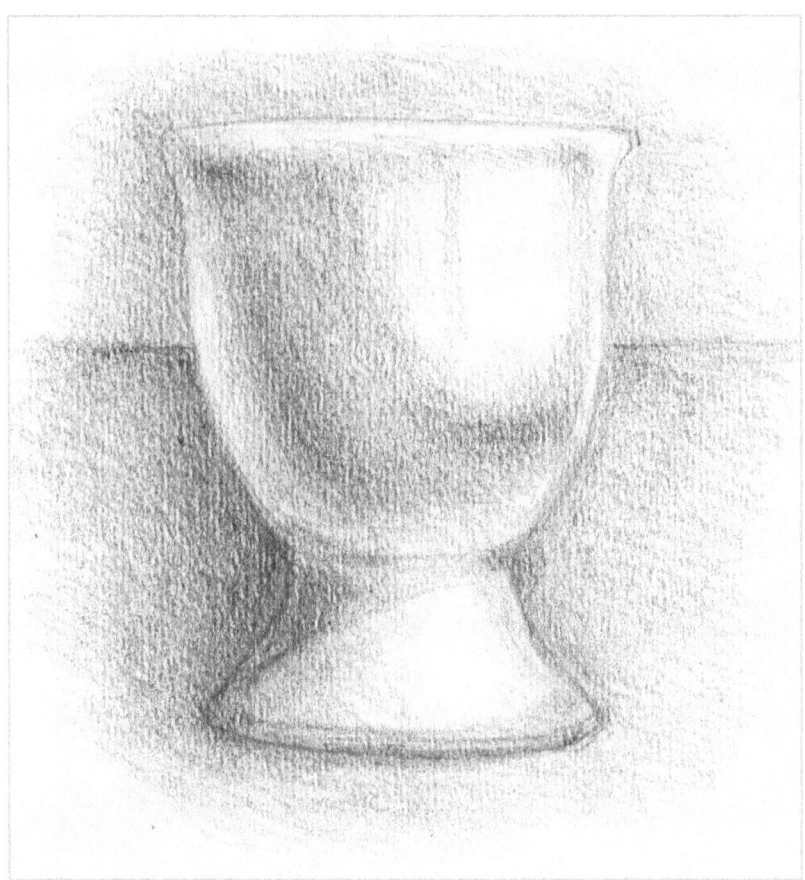

Guidance: Shading required here is of a more delicate nature. Begin with the darkest areas of the eggcup which are two dark bands on the main cup, but use light shading initially. Use the oblique edge of the pencil to obtain soft strokes. Work over the paler areas with light strokes, avoiding the areas of highlight. Work over the dark areas again for more depth, applying progressively lighter shading as you work outwards. Repeat this procedure, working a little darker each time to attain smooth gradations in tone. Use the same technique for the lower cone. Use the edge of the nib to attain a crisp outline to the shadow. The background can be filled in with more vigorous strokes to provide contrast in textures.

Chapter 10

Advanced Drawing Exercises

You might have realised that you have now exercised all five principles of drawing as you have worked through this book (edges, spaces, relationships, tone and the whole picture).

You have also exercised the right-brain and subdued the left-brain as you have gone through the exercises within this book. You may have discovered your own way of working during your practice and your own drawing style is emerging. You may even feel inspired to explore other drawing mediums, which might be pastels, ink, charcoal or crayons. With this new learned skill in drawing, possibilities suddenly open out to you. You might feel it necessary to keep practicing the exercises or recap on one or two as a reminder.

When you are ready, you might like to try something more challenging. As a taster, I have provided a step-by-step instruction on how to shade a hypothetical sphere, which can be practiced anywhere whether or not a spherical object is handy or if the lighting conditions are right. This might serve a useful bridging exercise into more advanced shading, which can be found within the latter half of this chapter.

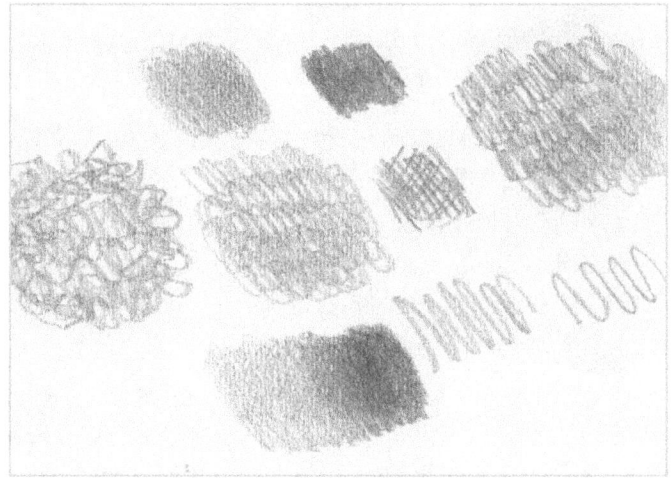

73

The Orb

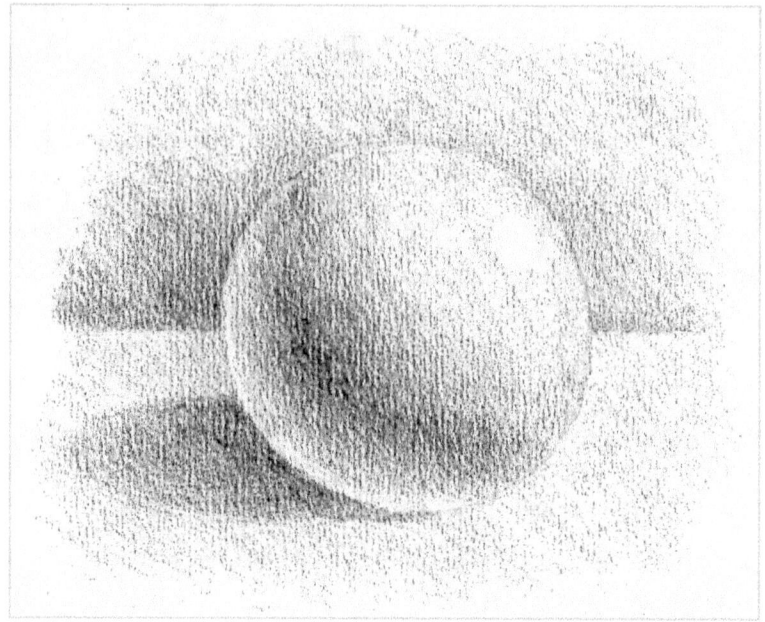

Instructions

1 Roughly in the centre of the page, faintly draw a circle approximately the width of your fist. Attain perfection as practiced in chapter 3, 'perfecting a circle in stages.' Once the circle is as accurate as you can make it, faintly draw a horizontal line on either side of this 'orb' to represent a resting surface. Use a ruler if necessary.

2 Very faintly, draw a small circular shape near the top right of the sphere. This is to represent the highlight. Be careful not to apply shading there when shading over the sphere.

3 To the left of the sphere, roughly three-quarters of the way across, draw a very faint 'C' shape to echo the contour of the sphere. This is to represent a dark crescent of shadow.

4 with the soft pencil, shade the background to the sphere, aiming for a pale grey tone. Move the nib of the pencil in roughly the same directions, keeping the lines soft. Allow this shading to fade out towards the edges.

5 Shade the tabletop a little paler than the background in step 4.

6 Shade as lightly as possible over the sphere, avoiding the circular highlight shape described in step 2. Aim for evenness in tone.

7 Now working from the 'C' shape described in step 3, shade a little darker here, tapering off to either side, aiming for a very fuzzy crescent shape.

8 Repeat step 7 beginning a little darker this time. Like paint, pencil shading is best applied in layers rather than in one go, working a little darker each time. Work lighter towards the highlight and to the far left of the orb. The latter is to represent reflected light – light reflected back into shadow from a neighbouring bright surface. Work in small circular strokes, aiming for a seamless finish. You may need to repeat this step a further two or three times to add depth and smoothness to the shading.

9 Now draw a flattened 'C' shape extending to the left of the orb to represent the shadow cast over the tabletop. Use the illustration as a guide. Again, start light, and then darker. Aim for a slightly darker shade near the orb than further

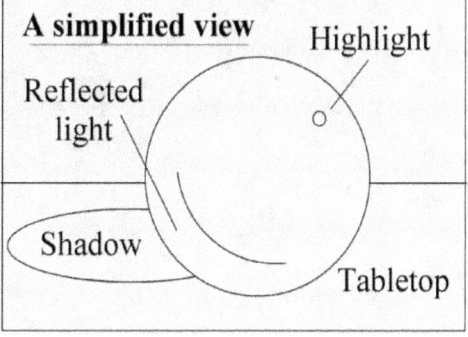

away. Practice this exercise as often as you wish. Aim for smooth gradations within the orb, getting the tonal balances right.

Advanced Shading

The following images feature more challenging subject matter for you to try. They are ordered from the simple. Don't worry if your drawing doesn't work out straightaway. Have another go on a separate day. Remember to practice the A, B and C of drawing and the basics of shading. Prior to shading, look for the negative shapes around the object to get the contours right. I have provided some tips with each image.

The Onion

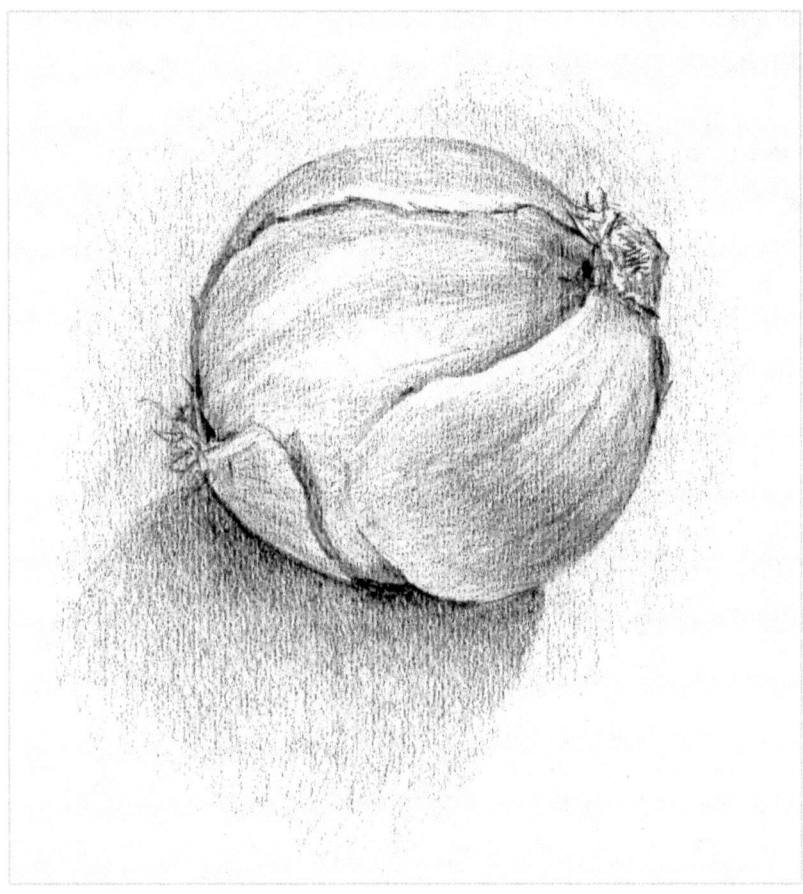

Guidance: The principles of shading this onion are roughly the same as shading the orb. Notice reflected light on the underside of the onion, and highlights on the upper portions.

Take care not to shade over the highlights and only very lightly over the reflected light. Once you have applied the preliminary shading, you can work over it, adding depth and achieving a smooth finish. Bear in mind the 'weight of lines' exercises in chapter 8 to suggest detail and textures on the skin. Apply the finest detail last, keeping the pencil sharp for crisp lines and edging.

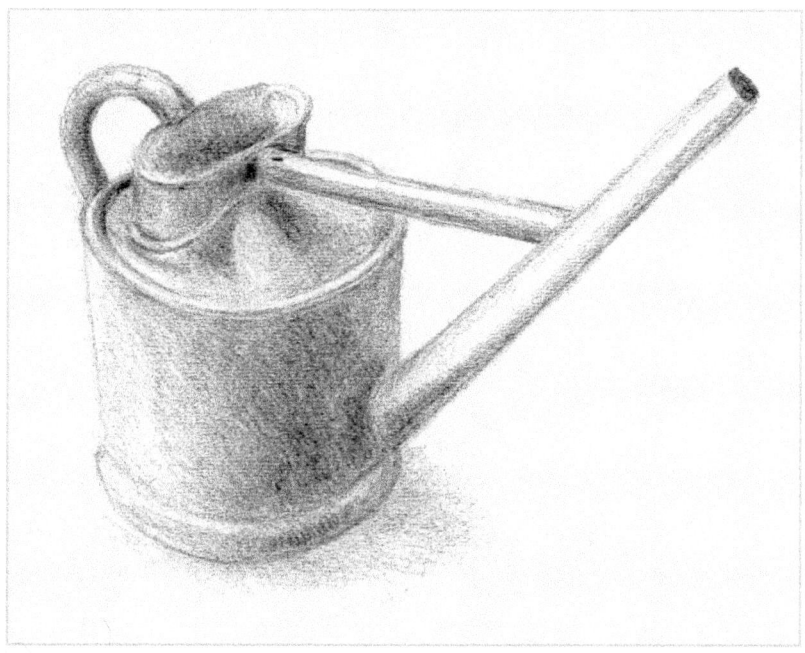

Guidance: Prepare the watering-can's sketch via the exercise on upside-drawing and negative space, as shown in chapters 5 and 6.

Most of the can's front comprises a large area of delicate tonal gradations. Practice delicate shading as shown within the orb and the eggcup. Work lightly at first, applying progressively more pressure each time you work over the object in layers.

The challenge lies in the elliptical areas around the top of the can. Notice the ellipses' tops are slightly paler in shade than the sides. The lips' edges exhibit a narrow dark band which wavers in tone along the way. Sharpen the pencil to apply detail around these areas and the handle. The weight of marks is relevant here.

Apply slightly darker shading only where it is needed. If you have trouble drawing ellipses, chapter 12 offers guidance.

The Scissors

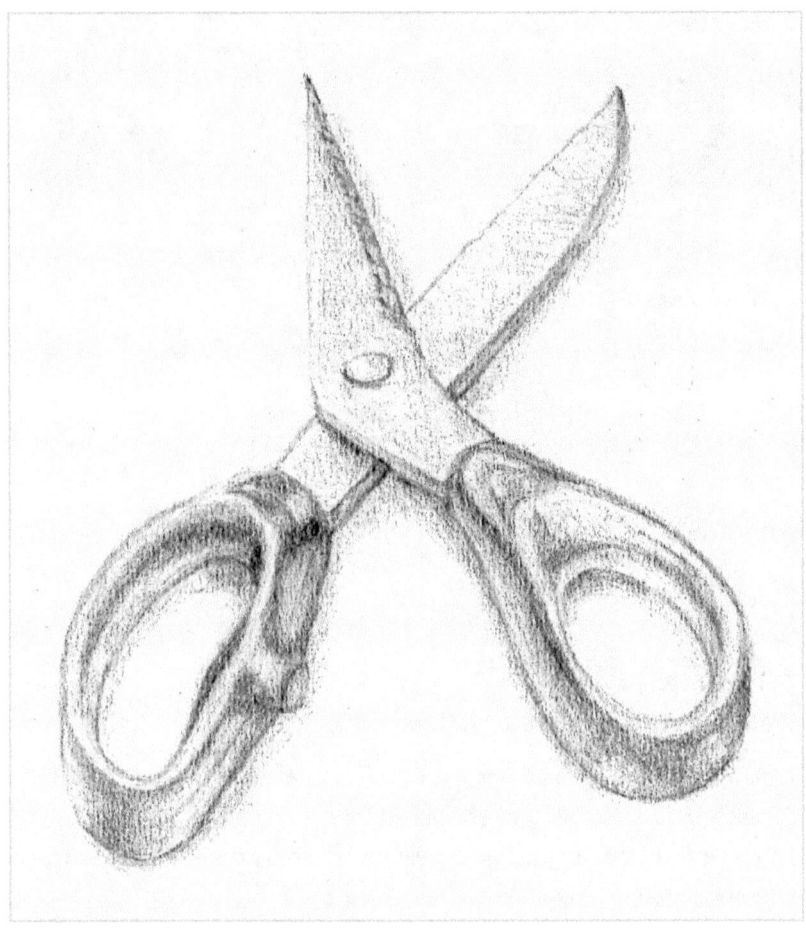

Guidance: The toughest part of this drawing will be the scissors' handles, which comprise a series of complex and irregular ellipses (like the Watering Can earlier). Embark upon the drawing here first, whilst feeling most up to the challenge.

Pay attention to the various bands of light and shadow, some of which disappear from view. Keep the tones soft and pale around the highlights. The blades exhibit mostly one tone which can be applied with soft, horizontal strokes.

Gardening Gloves

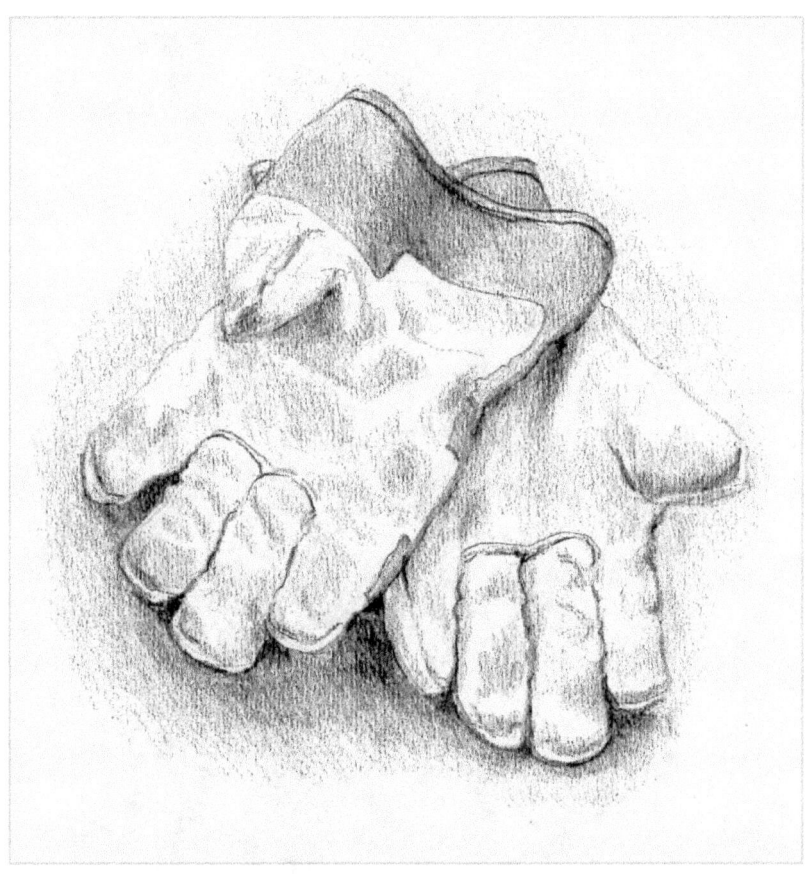

Guidance: These gardening gloves comprise an array of complex tones, but really, the main body of the gloves consists roughly of two tones: pale and highlight. Some artists may shade the gloves with one tone and then 'draw' highlights with the edge of a putty rubber. You may try this technique too, but use a rubber with a sharp edge to 'cut' into the shading.

View the highlights as a network of pales against a slightly-shaded ground. Apply shadows last, edging the gloves and illustrating stitches with a sharp pencil. Shade out from beneath the gloves.

The Coffee-grinder

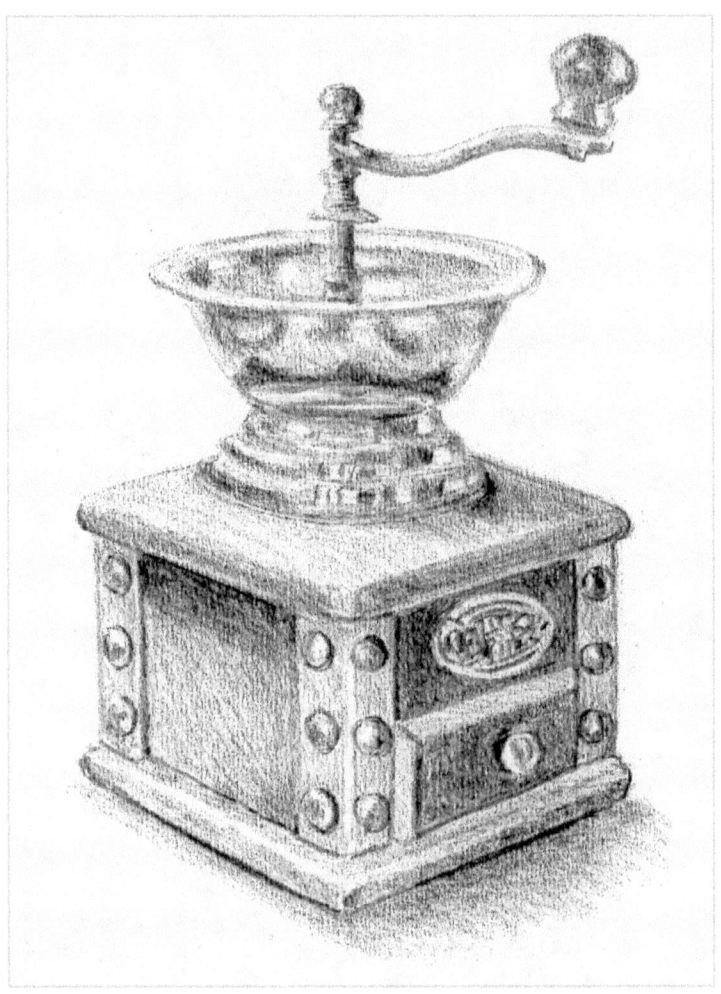

Guidance: this coffee-grinder echoes the exercise on shading a cube earlier in this chapter. Suggest form by breaking the object down into four or five tonal areas before working in detail. Once these tonal shapes have been applied, work on the studs and the label via a sharp pencil. The main challenge lies in the metallic funnel at the top. Pay particular attention to the series of reflections around the base of the bowl which feature abstract shapes.

The Drinking Glass

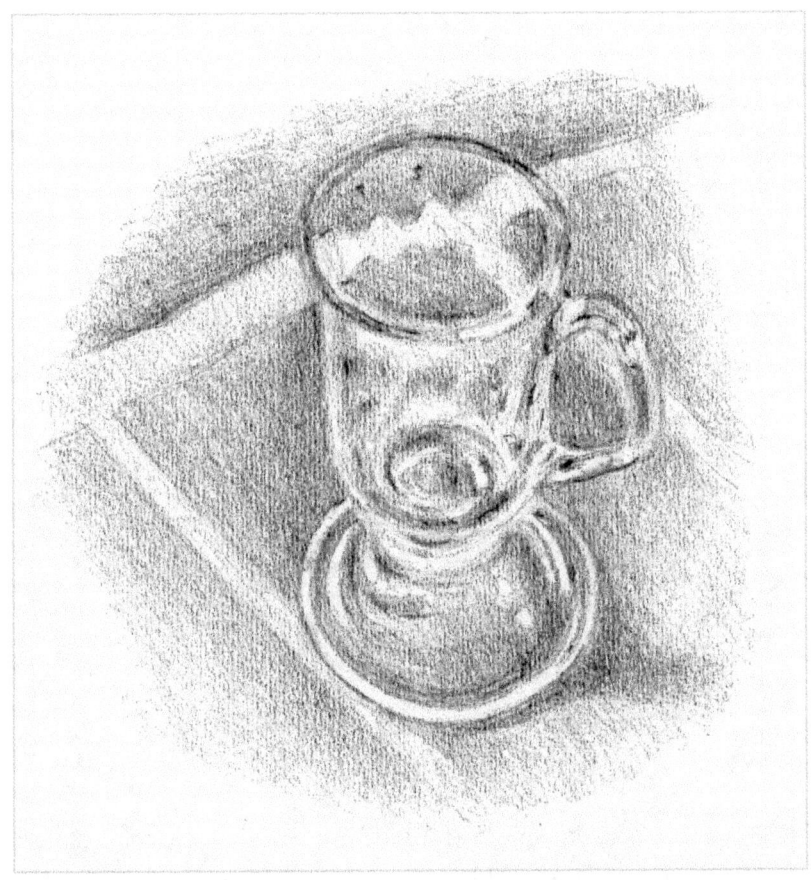

Guidance: Not only does this glass exhibit foreshortening but also a complex soupcon of reflections around the base of the glass. Begin by observing symmetrical drawing as demonstrated in chapter 3. Set the scene by shading in the background around the glass first. Express distortions of the background through the glass. The main challenge lies in the glass itself. Break down these subtle shifts in tones by viewing them as circular pale and dark bands. Keep the pencil sharp for detail around the highlights and for edging.

Abstract drawing and the weight of marks (chapters 4 and 8) particularly applies in this drawing exercise.

Chapter 11

Shading on Grey Paper

Working on grey paper instead of white is great for producing tonal studies, as you can work from highlights first-off instead of the dark tones. This makes tones easier to measure against one another.

I used Ingres paper (named after French artist Dominique-Ingres) a mid-toned paper with a regular canvas-like texture, available from eggshell to grey. However, you may use any grey paper that suits you when following the demonstrations within this chapter.

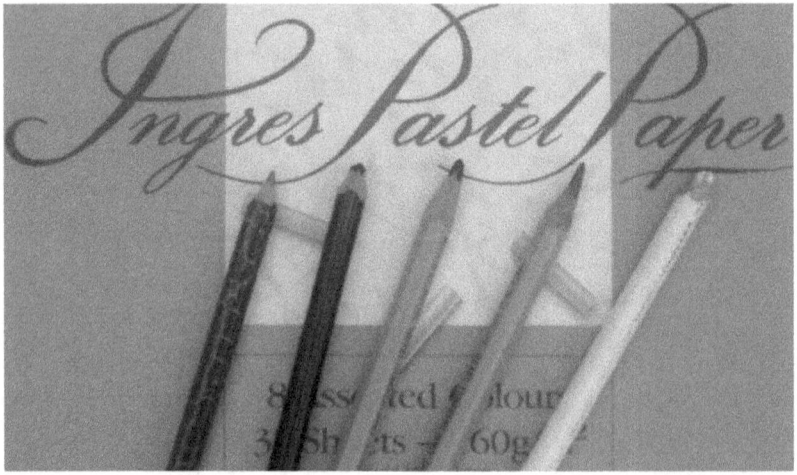

The image above shows a pad of Ingres paper and the pencils used for the following demonstrations. From the left, a HB pencil, a black pastel pencil, a black watercolor pencil, Paynes grey watercolor pencil and a white pastel pencil.

The HB pencil was used for the under-drawing. I did not add water to the watercolour pencils as I could have, but used them for their stability and robustness during shading. The nibs do not wear down too quickly and can be sharpened to a fine point for detail. Pastel pencils offer more depth in tone, but are more prone to smudging and wearing down during the shading.

Pastel Effects

Various tonal effects can be achieved with just these five pencils as can be seen on the image below. Try out different soft pencils by allowing the nib to 'skid' over the surface for soft effects, or by pressing the nib down for definite lines.

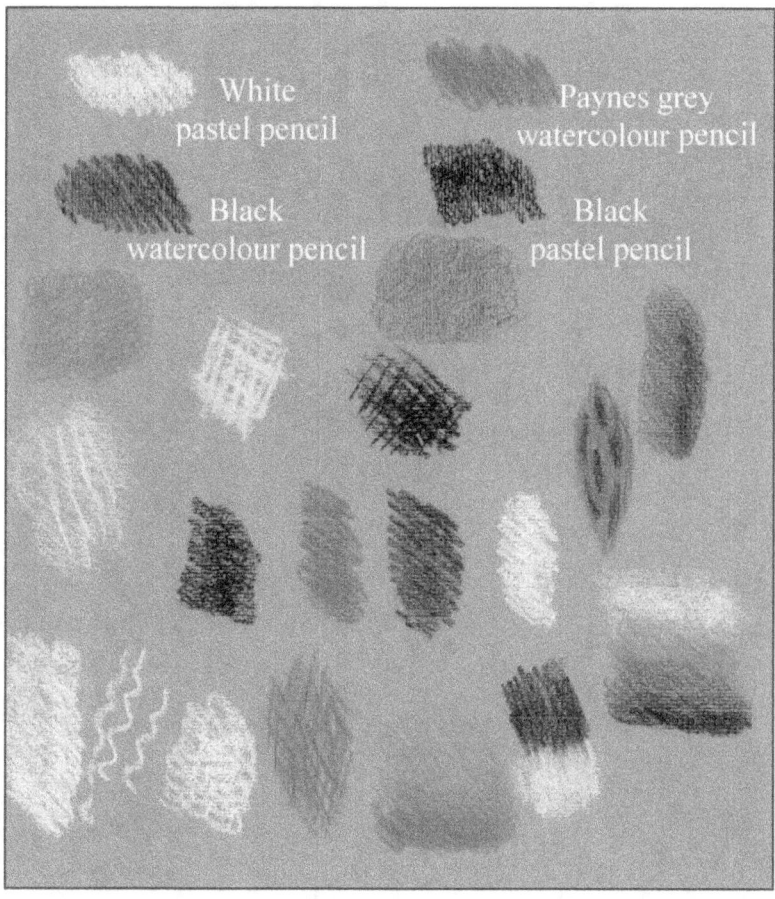

Try moving the pencil in different directions to create crosshatches, swirls or solid areas of tone. Using a combination of pencils in one area can create further interesting effects

Canada Goose

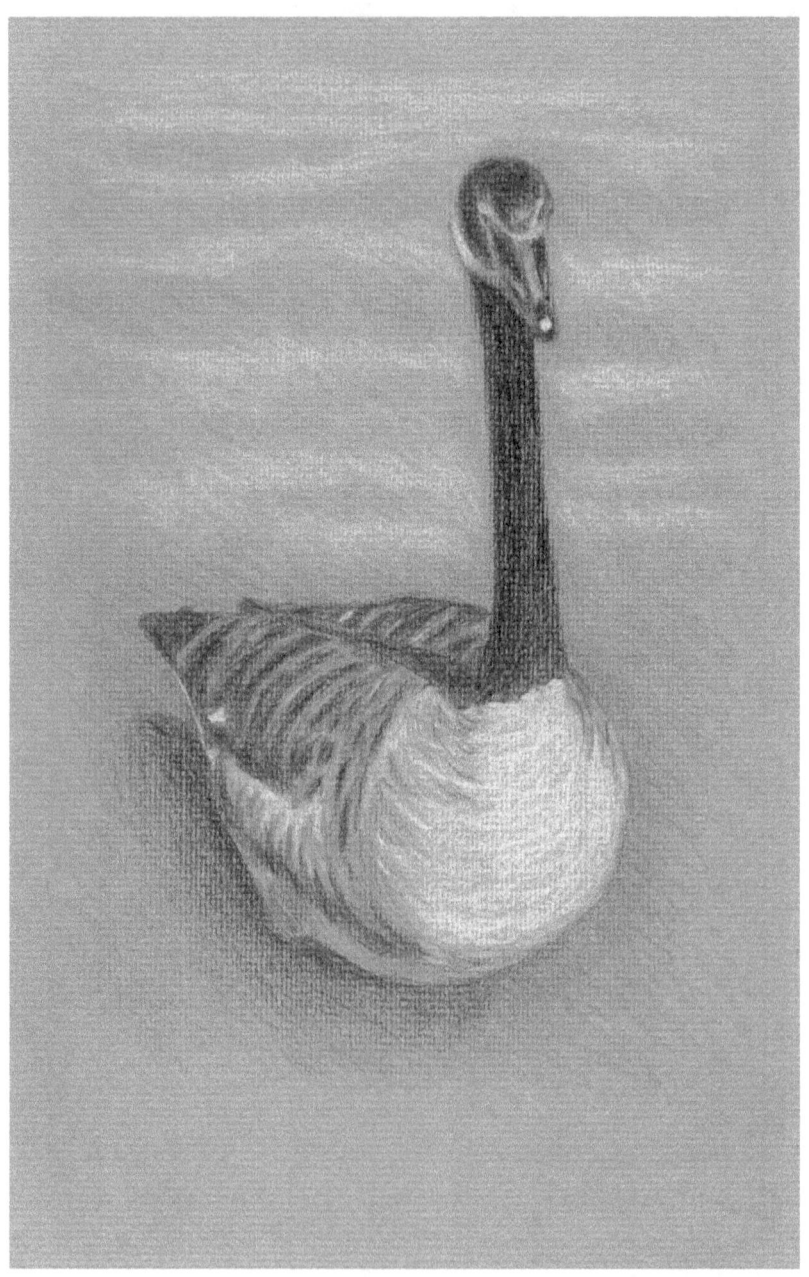

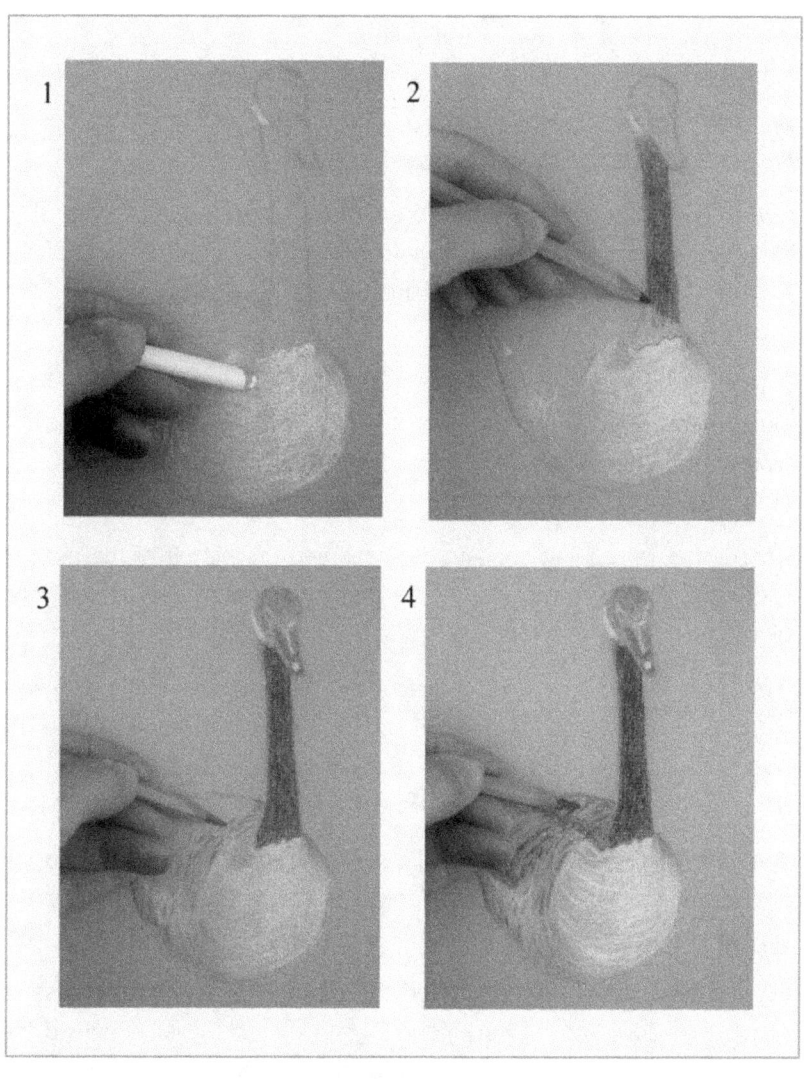

Challenge: A combination of shading techniques has been used to capture the textures of the bird. This includes a fair amount of detail on the plumage and face. But soft shading has been used for the bird's breast and the background. This means the pencils have been used in various ways. Care is therefore needed not to use the same approach for the entire drawing.

The Method

1 I made a light sketch of the bird with a HB pencil prior to shading. I began with the bird's white plumage at its chest. I applied fine strokes via the white chalk pastel pencil to express the highlights.

I worked the pencil in the direction of the feathers, across the chest in loose arcs. I allowed some streaks to remain to suggest texture of the feathers. I then dabbed a few highlights to the bird's beak and eyes with more solid areas of tone.

2 With the black watercolour pencil, I shaded in the neck of the goose, aiming for smooth coverage. Do not press the pencil too hard initially. I worked over the area a few times, achieving an ever darker tone each time.

I applied extra shading beneath the beak and on the left of the neck to suggest form. I then worked carefully over the goose's head, avoiding the highlighted areas.

3 With the Paynes grey pencil I sketched in the markings on the plumage, working back towards the tail in a sort of fish scale pattern. I made the lines sufficiently bold so that I could easily shade between them with a darker pencil and yet retain a loose shading style.

4 With the black watercolour pencil, I worked around the grey markings on the goose's feathers. I added a shadow area behind the neck, to create the illusion of light.

For the bird's final touch, I worked the dark pencil around the base to suggest shadow. For the background, I shaded soft wavelets behind the bird with the chalk pencil. I used the black watercolour pencil very lightly between these soft highlights to bring out form in the waves.

Roman Bust

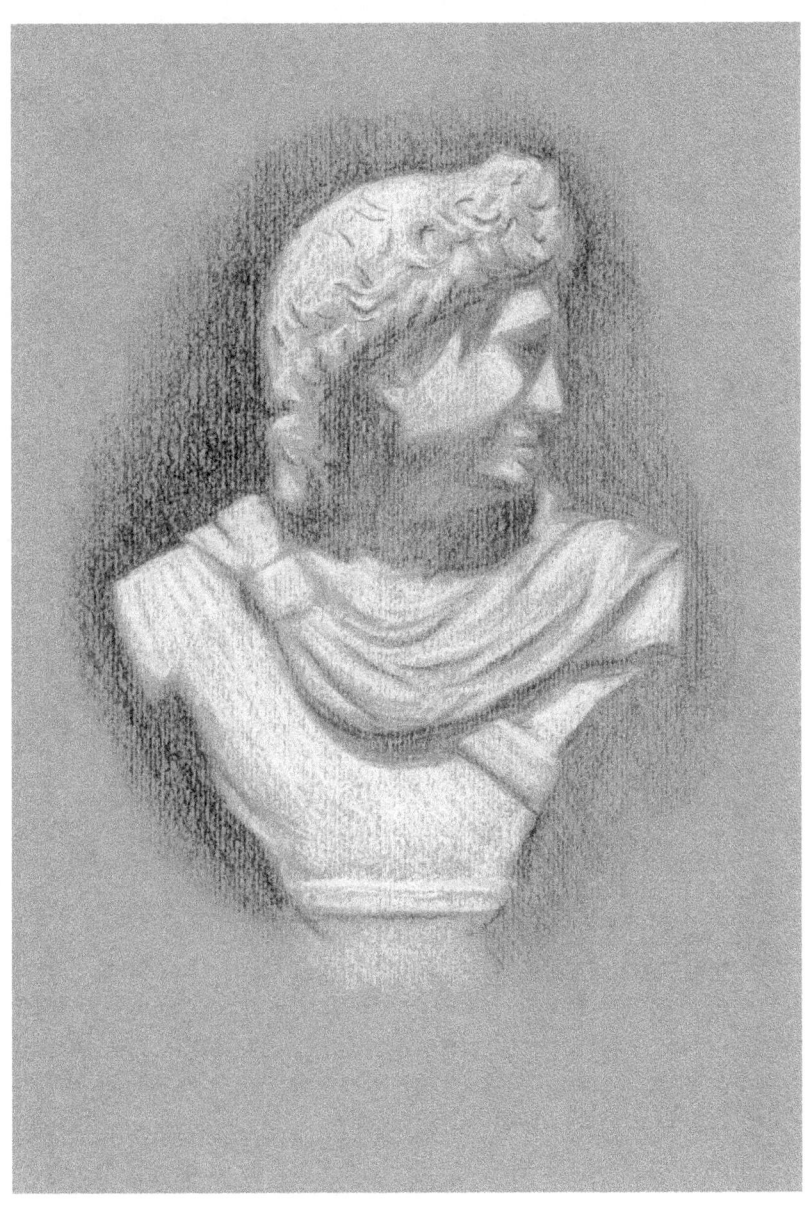

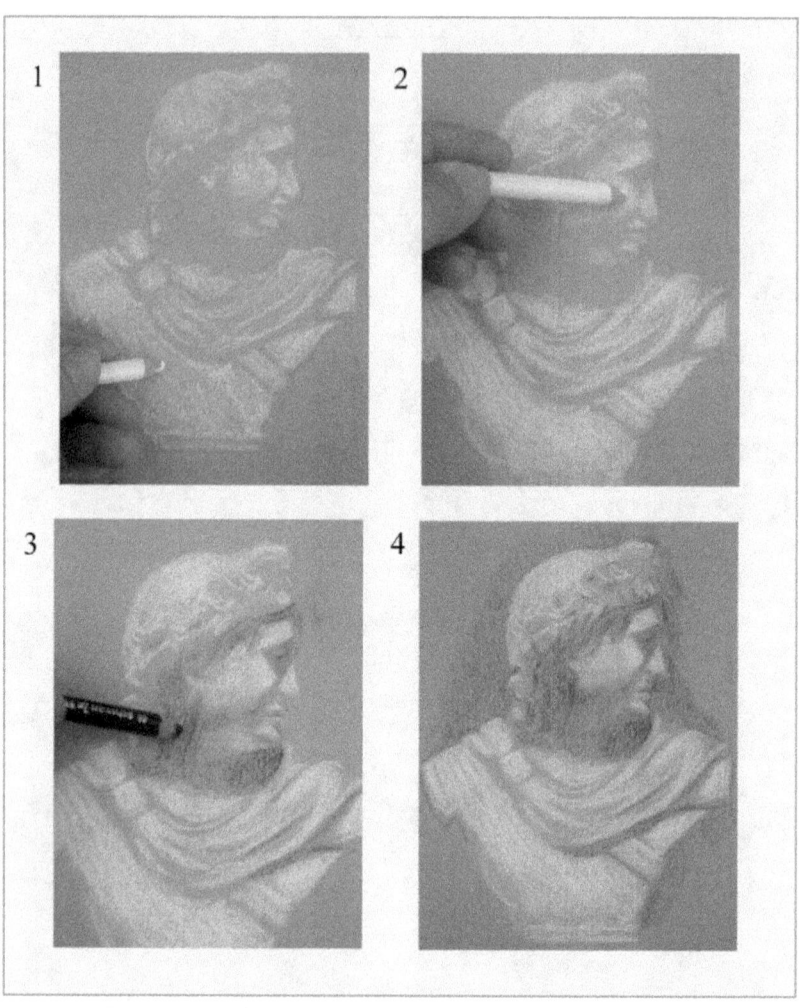

Challenge: Due to neighbouring bright surfaces, this statue exhibits a lot of reflected light (light within shadow). Care is needed not to go over these areas or the shadows will appear overly-harsh and black. The drapery could confound with its complex folds. The secret is to break down each area into abstract forms and to work lightly at first.

The Method

1 I made a light sketch with a HB pencil before embarking the shading. With a white chalk pastel.

I began applying soft highlights to the statue, allowing the grey paper to show through where the shadows will be. I worked the pencil lightly and with broad strokes enabling me to express further highlights.

2 I applied a little more pressure onto the chalk pastel to express solid highlights around the upper cheekbone, nose and crown. I used linear strokes around the drapery to bring out form.

To ensure accuracy, I turned the image and the drawing upside down. This helped to bring an abstract quality to the areas of light and shadow.

3 I applied soft shading with the black pastel pencil, working over the most subtle shadows first. There is a little reflected light beneath the chin, so I kept the tones light here.

I worked over the rest of the statue, using the same soft shading, working a little darker around the left shoulder, eye socket, hairline and the lower drapery.

4 I introduced a little detail around the hair, moving the dark pastel in light swirls. I then reinforced the shadows on the underside of the drapery.

Finally, I moved the pastel gently over the background to create stark contrast between light and dark and to enhance the effect of sunlight bouncing off the statue.

Chapter 12

When Rules Apply

The focus of the book has been upon promoting the right-brain during drawing. The right-brain, as we have seen, is instinctive, non-verbal and sees the big picture – the qualities needed for drawing truthfully. But the left-brain is often required for calculating the angle of a receding edge or drawing an ellipse. This chapter is therefore dedicated to certain rules that apply in drawing.

If you learn to draw what you see, not what you think you see, the drawing will work out by itself. But some understanding of vanishing points and plotting measurements will come in useful when presented with a scene full of buildings or a still life. Ellipses, for example, have often proved troublesome if not observed properly. Let's take a look at when rules apply in drawing. The following subsections within this chapter tackle various areas in drawing regarding working out accuracy.

- Part: I The viewfinder
- Part: II Plotting your drawing
- Part: III Perspectives made simple
- Part: IV Ellipses without corners

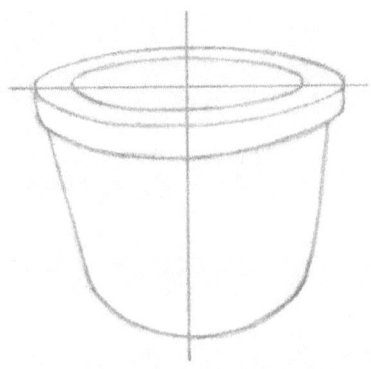

Part I

The Viewfinder

A tool known as the artist's viewfinder is a piece of card with a window cut into it. Like a camera's viewfinder, it can cut out surrounding elements when looking for compositions. The viewfinder can also be used to plot a drawing, as negative space is easier to see. You might find it a useful tool when trying out the exercises in chapter 5: a picture within a frame. Instructions on how to use the viewfinder will follow this demonstration.

You may create a viewfinder simply by cutting a square hole into a piece of paper. For a more robust type, you will need the following materials as shown in picture **1** of the following page:

1. A cutting mat or old magazines to cut on
2. A piece of card measuring 11 x 8 inches (20 x 28cm)
3. Scissors
4. Scalpel
5. Pencil
6. A steel ruler
7. Double sided cellotape
8. Cotton

Making the Viewfinder

2 Cut the card equally in half so that each measures.5.5 x 8 inches (14x20cm) and then draw a cross in the centre of each piece of card.

3 Carefully cut a rectangular hole in the centre of each card measuring 2.5 x 3 inches (6 x 7.5 cm). These proportions will match most standard sketchbook sizes.

4 Secure the cotton thread via the tape to the centre-point of an edge of the window and carefully stretch it across the window to the opposing edge. Place another piece of thread across the centre-point of the top and bottom of the window. The thread should now form a cross over the window from central points.

5 The other piece of card can be fixed on top, sandwiching the edges of the cotton between the two via the double-sided cellotape.

6 Ensure the two pieces of card are stuck fast. Trim excess cotton from the edges. The viewfinder is ready for use.

<u>Making the Viewfinder</u>

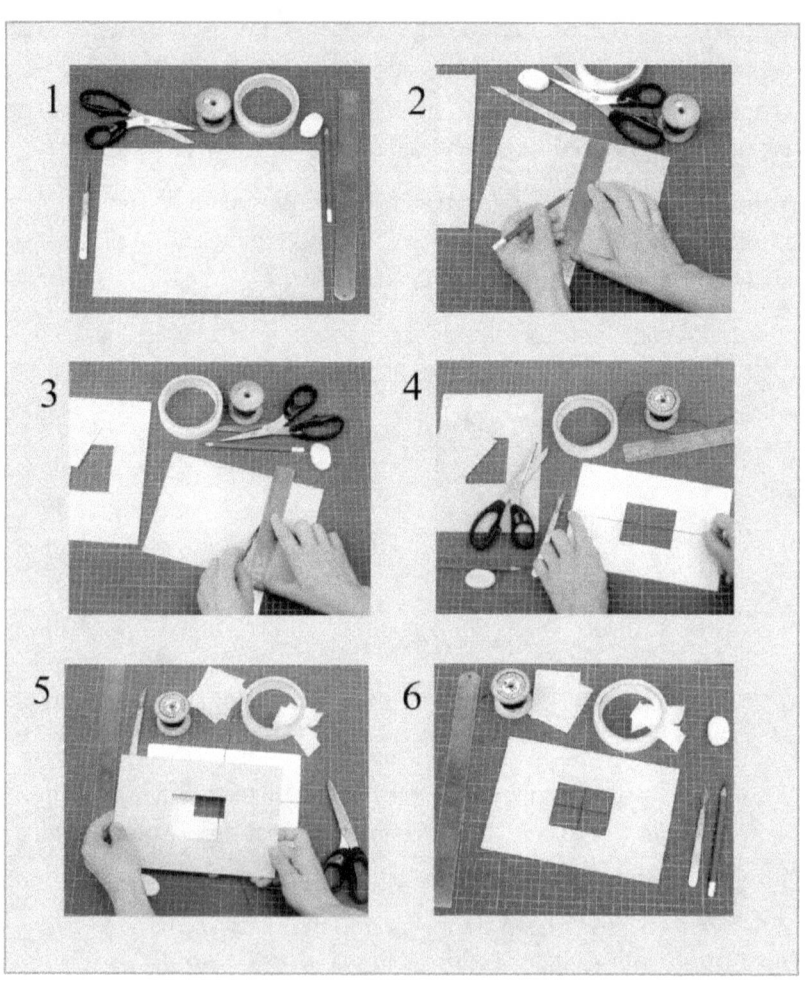

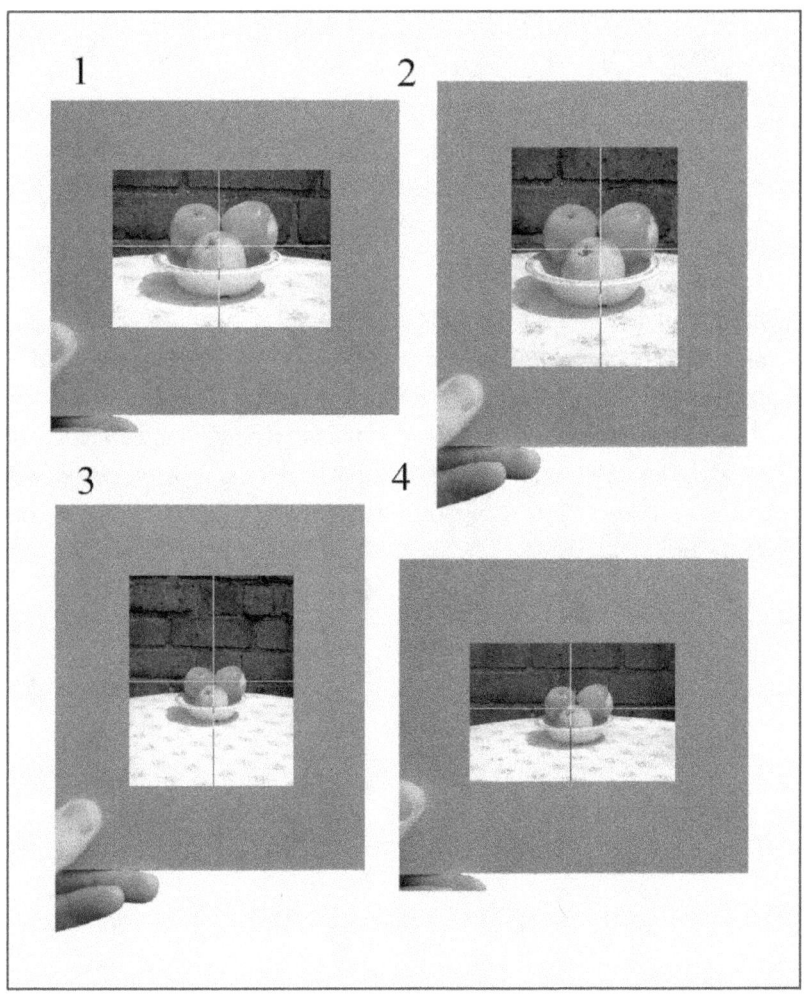

The viewfinder acts like a frame from which compositions can be found. By closing one eye and peeking through the window, an edited version of the world can be seen.

1 By holding the viewfinder in landscape mode, the width of the composition will be emphasized. **2** By holding the viewfinder in portrait mode, the top and bottom of the view will be emphasized. By moving the frame away from the eye, the view zooms in on an object, as can be seen in the aforementioned two images. By moving the viewfinder towards the eye, a wider perspective of the world can be seen, as can be seen in the lower images, **3** and **4**.

The cross over the window serves as a plotting guide when it comes to deciphering the centre-point of the view and working out how objects lie within each quadrant. This makes the viewfinder an ideal drawing aid.

You may try a simplified drawing of what can be seen through the aperture by transferring this image onto the drawing surface. Holding the viewfinder steadily will ensure consistency. Anything can be sketched at hand; a chair, a still life or a view through a window. The aim is to simply sketch a series of lines as seen through the viewfinder. The viewfinder will also reveal an interesting composition that may otherwise be overlooked with the naked eye. This is because the window can be used to filter out information.

Part II

Plotting your Drawing

Various methods can be used to plot your drawing. Two methods are outlined here. They can be used in isolation or together.

The first method of plotting, shown in **fig 1** of the following page, involves holding up a pencil to eye-level and positioning it at a fixed distance from your eye. Close one eye to eradicate the parallax view. You can then use the tip of the pencil to mark an edge of a subject matter and then slide your thumb along the pencil to take a measurement. Care is needed not to alter the distance between pencil and eye or the measurements will not be reliable.

Start with large elements and work down to the small by taking measurements with the pencil. Identify a "key" measurement within the composition starting with the biggest. This could be the height of a jug or the width of an apple. This "key" may be used as a foundation from which to build up the sketch and make comparisons with other aspects of the composition. The pot in fig 1, for instance equals the width of the pepper. Other key measurements can be found and plotted onto the page. Always start with the largest element within the drawing and then work down to the smaller ones.

The second method of plotting shown in **fig 2** on the following page can be used in conjunction with the viewfinder described previously, although using one is not essential. Make a visual estimate of the proportions of your composition (whether it is wide, narrow or square). Draw a margin around the edges of the page to reflect these proportions. Draw a faint cross in the centre as shown. The aim is to use these quadrants to scale up the drawing so that it sits centrally on the page. This will guard against drawing too small or off-centre on the page.

The viewfinder can help make this method of drawing easier, as the view is divided into quadrants and contained within a frame. The size and shape of each object can be checked for accuracy against the drawing.

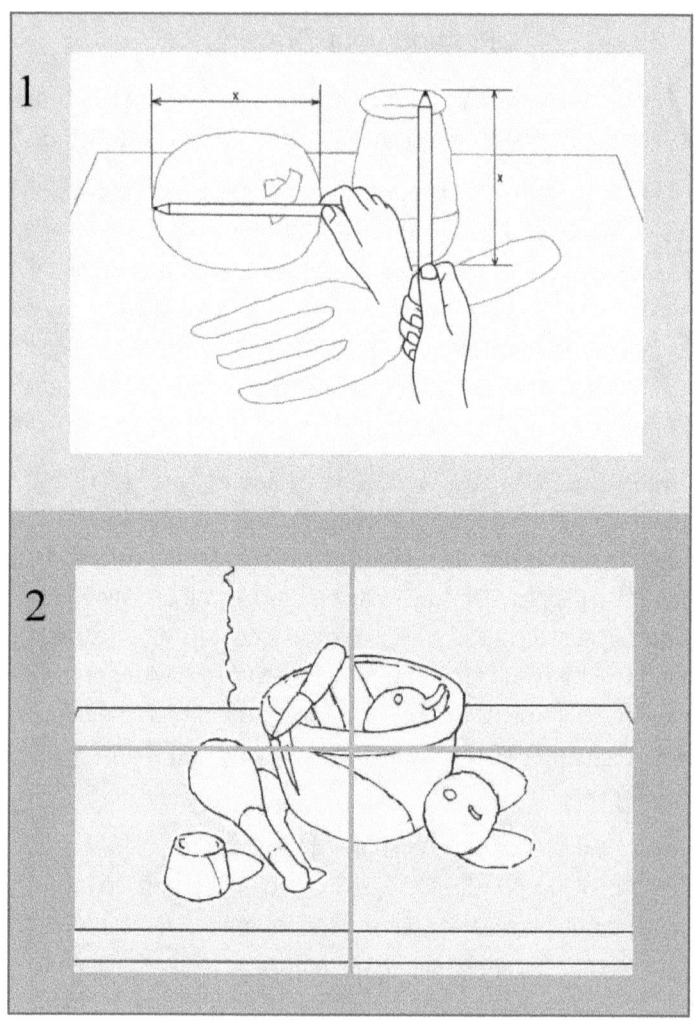

1 shows how a drawing can be plotted by holding the pencil at a fixed distance from the eye and taking relative measurements starting with the largest. **2** show how the drawing can be plotted by visually judging what lie within each quadrant of the composition and then transferring this information onto the page. The viewfinder can be used as a resource for this method of plotting.

Part III

Vanishing Points Made Simple

Anyone who struggles with perspectives may feel dismay at the mention of vanishing points. Objects possessing receding edges such as cubes, buildings and railway tracks are the subjects to be avoided in drawing. However, without some understanding of these theories, solutions to a drawing problem are less likely to be found. Take a look at the following cubes and railway tracks. Can you define the problem with each one? Answers can be found afterwards.

<u>Impossible Angles</u>

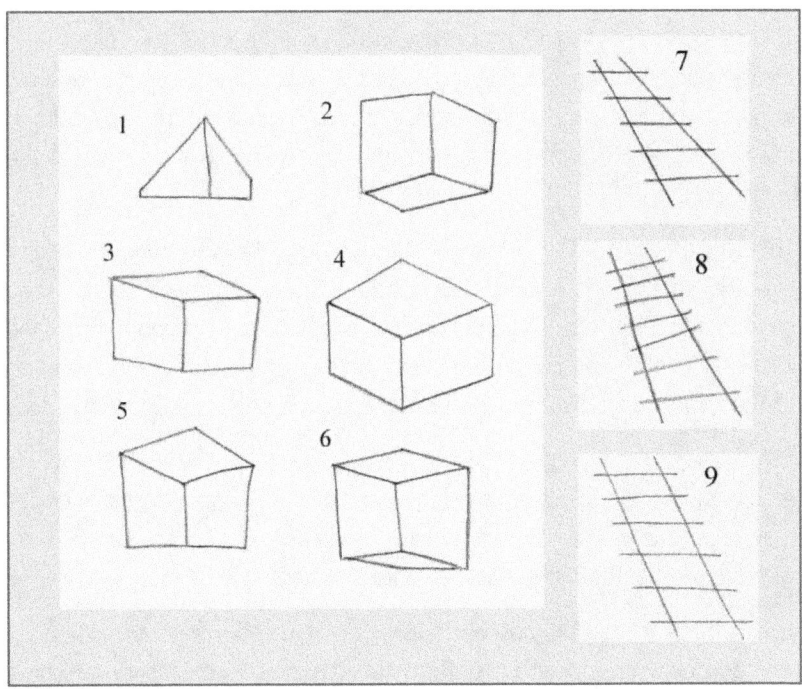

1 shows a cube with edges that recede too steeply to make sense. 2 shows a cube with faces that are not parallel with one another, creating a 'wedged' effect. 3 shows a cube with edges that do not appear to recede with distance. 4 shows a cube where the upper face appears skewed in

relation to the bottom face. **5** shows a cube resting on a flat surface, yet the upper face is almost facing us. **6** shows a cube where both upper and lower faces can be seen simultaneously. This is impossible.

Now for the tracks. In **7**, the runners on the track are equally spaced apart where the distance between each should appear to decrease with distance. In **8** the track appears buckled as the runners are not horizontal in formation. In **9**, the track lines are running parallel with one another, where they should appear to converge with distance.

Most of these figures do not possess a vanishing point. But what is the vanishing point?

The Vanishing Point

Take a look at any object that possesses a straight edge. This might be a railway track, a building or indeed a cube. If any of these edges continued to recede on and on into the distance, it would eventually reach a point at the horizon where the straight edge appears to end. This is known at the vanishing point.

The illustration on the following page shows the vanishing points of hypothetical cuboids resting on a tabletop. The horizon line can be seen beyond the tabletop. This horizon line is a visible (or hypothetical) line located straight ahead and situated at eyelevel of the viewer. The location of the cuboid in relation to the horizon line will determine how its edges recede.

As can be seen in the illustration, the cuboid on the right possesses edges that recede downwards *and* upwards towards this hypothetical horizon where they eventually meet at the vanishing point.

The cuboid on the left possesses edges that recede *only* upwards, as it located below the horizon line. Both cuboids possess their own vanishing points. Take note, the further edge of the tabletop and the horizon line is not the same thing.

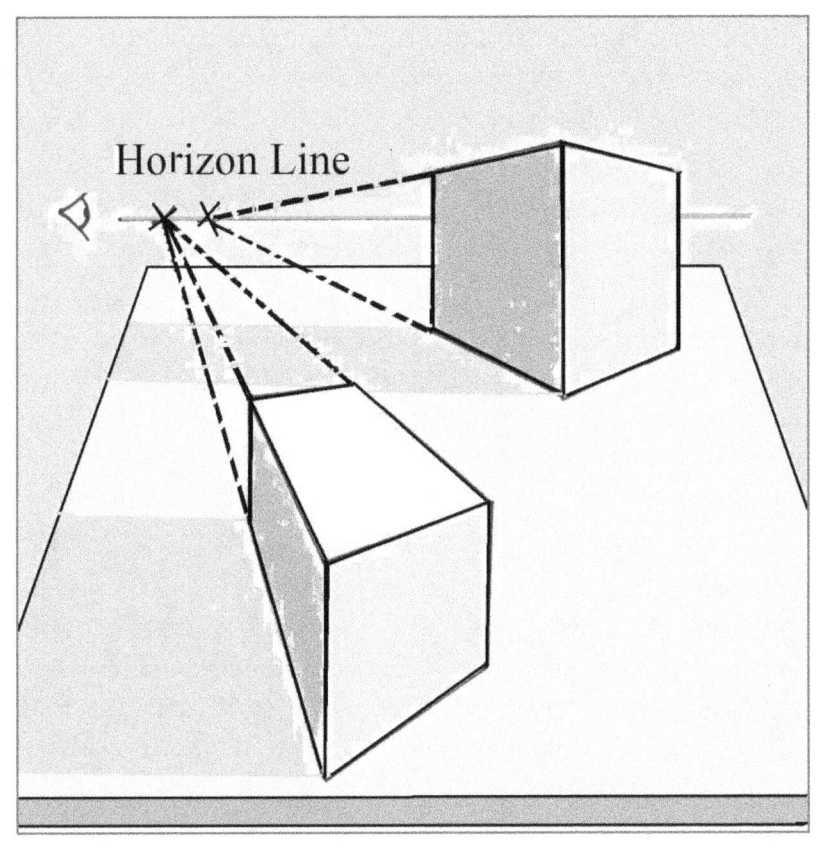

Plotting Angles for Buildings

Now for something more complex. The following step by step demonstration illustrates how to plot the receding angles and vanishing points to a series of buildings. Images can be found after these instructions.

1 I worked out how large I wanted the drawing to be on the paper via the plotting method described in part II of this chapter (you may employ a viewfinder as described in part I). The height of the church for example is roughly the same as the composition's width, so the composition will be square and the centre-point easily worked out.

I then established the proportions of the buildings by looking for measurements in common. The width of the church tower equals half its height. The annex building extending to the left of the image is half as high as it is long.

Not every measurement will fit so neatly, so 'almost' or 'roughly' will often have to suffice when comparing one with the other.

2 The vanishing point is a location on the horizon where apparently converging edges from a structure such as a building or a road meets. The church having two visible sides exhibits two vanishing points on either side as can be seen in the picture. The bottom and the top edge of the church will angle away towards the horizon until both meet. Every building will generate its own vanishing point(s).

The location of the horizon line is important here, as it determines the steepness of the angles of receding edges. Any aspect of the building that falls below the horizon line will generate angles that appear to recede *upwards* towards a vanishing point, as can be seen from the base of the church. A structure that lies above the horizon, such as the top of the church tower, will generate angles that appear to recede *downwards* towards the vanishing point.

Both hypothetical lines of a receding edge must meet on the horizon for the drawing to make sense.

3 Many buildings possess rustic contours and angles out of true, in which case, draftsman-like drawings will fail to capture the character of such buildings. This is why sensitive observation is always the key to effective drawing.

I injected some expression into the lines to reflect the age of the buildings and introduced detail into the trees. The lines of perspective however form the skeleton of this sketch.

Plotting Vanishing Points

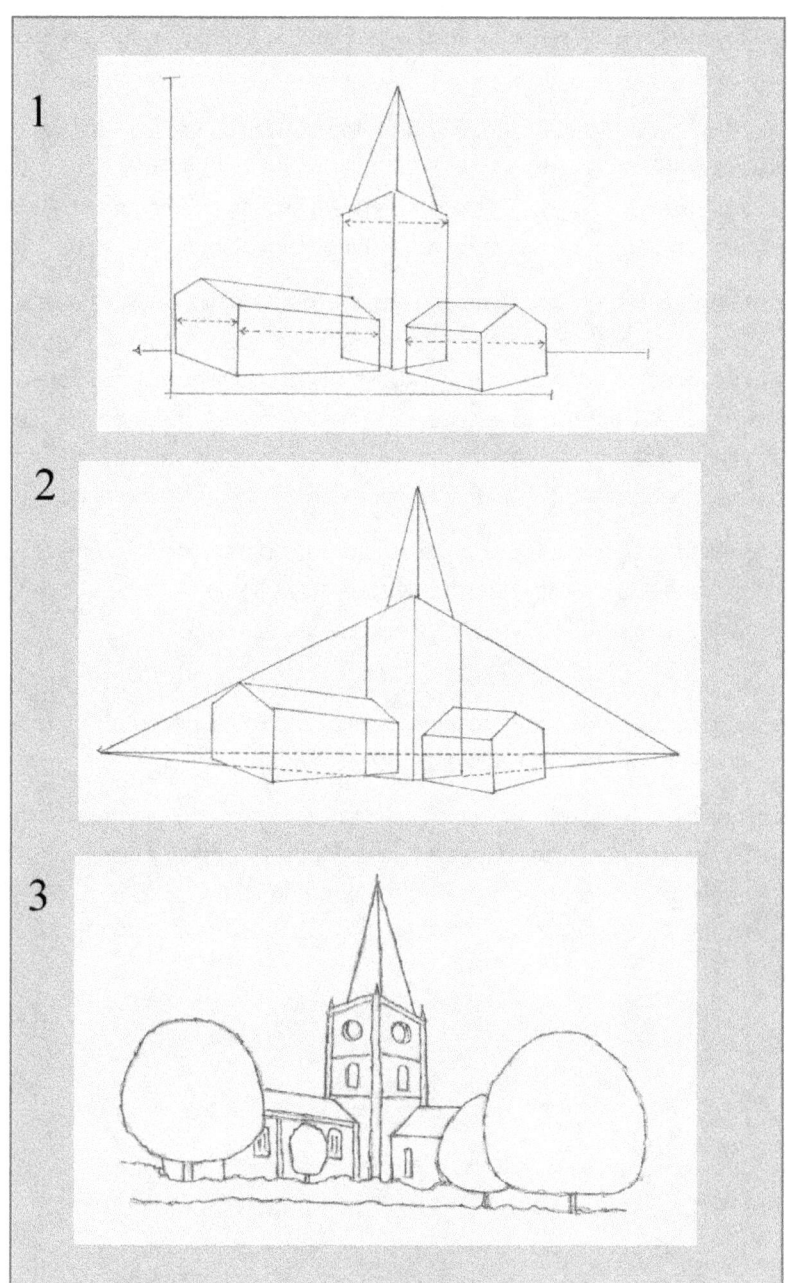

Where Lines Converge

The following points serve to recap what we have learned about vanishing points.

Observe how a receding straight edge slopes away, whether it is steep or shallow. If this receding edge went on forever, it would eventually reach a point on the horizon line. This point is known as the vanishing point. Every receding straight edge has its own vanishing point.

A straight receding edge that begins below this horizon line will generate an angle that will appear to recede *upwards* towards the horizon; a straight receding edge that begins above the horizon line will generate an angle that will appear to recede *downwards* towards the horizon. The receding edges of any perpendicular object will appear to converge towards one another with distance until it reaches the vanishing point.

A receding straight edge that appears near the horizon line will generate a shallow angle; a similar edge that is situated at some distance above or below the horizon line will generate a steep angle.

Detail on perpendicular objects such as patterns or text on boxes will appear to squash up and get thinner if on a receding surface. This includes the spaces between these elements.

But not all objects with perpendicular aspects have crisp corners. Some biscuit tins are dented or imperfect, and print may appear uneven. These imperfections will often add interest, realism and character to a still life or landscape.

Part IV

Ellipses without Corners

M any household objects contain ellipses such as vases and bottles, but drawing ellipses form a common difficulty. Can you identify the errors with the images on the right? Answers can be found on the following page.

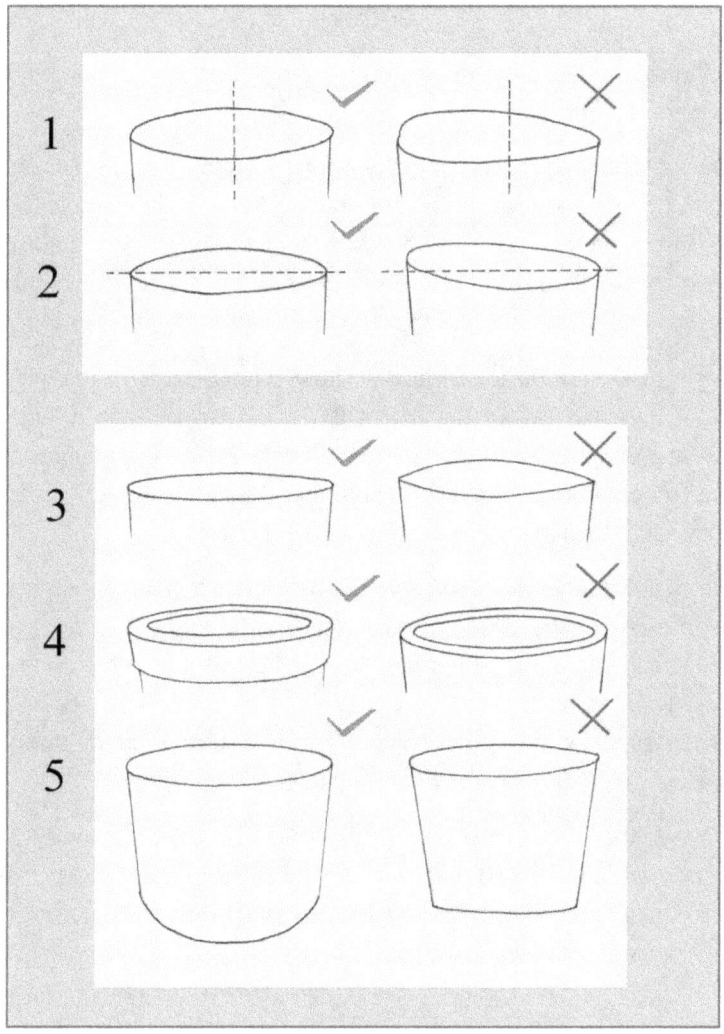

Images **1** and **2** shows asymmetrical ellipses, either being tear-shaped or sloping to one side. **3** show an ellipse with corners. In **4** the rim of the ellipse is the same width on all sides, creating a doughnut shape. And **5** shows a flat bottom to an object with an open ellipse.

All the aforementioned are common errors that occur when drawing ellipses. What is the best way to draw an ellipse? Drawing a hypothetical ellipse is a start. Here's how.

Guidance:

Supporting images follow these step by step instructions on how to draw an ellipse.

1 Draw a faint cross to aid symmetry as practiced in chapter 3. Ensure the cross is upright and level. If you are drawing from life, judge how "open" the ellipse is on the object. Is it almost fully open, like an oval; is it akin to an eye shape? Ensure the ellipse sits centrally on the cross and that its widest point is at the centre of the cross.

2 Begin to sketch the ellipse faintly. Draw curved edges to the left and right of the cross (where the rim of the object will be) and a flattened curve at the upper and lower part of the cross. Turn the image upside down to ensure it is symmetrical. Note that the further curve will appear slightly flatter than the nearer curve due to its proximity.

3 Sketch in the inner rim. Don't make the thickness of the rim the same all around (see following illustration for details). The further rim will appear slightly thinner than the nearer rim. Knit each element together using soft, curved lines. Stand back to view the ellipse as a whole to ensure it is symmetrical and that it curves softly. Turning the picture upside down will reveal deviances, unevenness or unwanted bends.

4 Observe the curve at the base of the cylindrical object or vessel. It will appear more pronounced than the curve of the ellipse at the top due to viewing the ellipse from above. Use the vertical line of the cross to plot the lowest point of the curve. Eradicate corners.

How to Draw an Ellipse

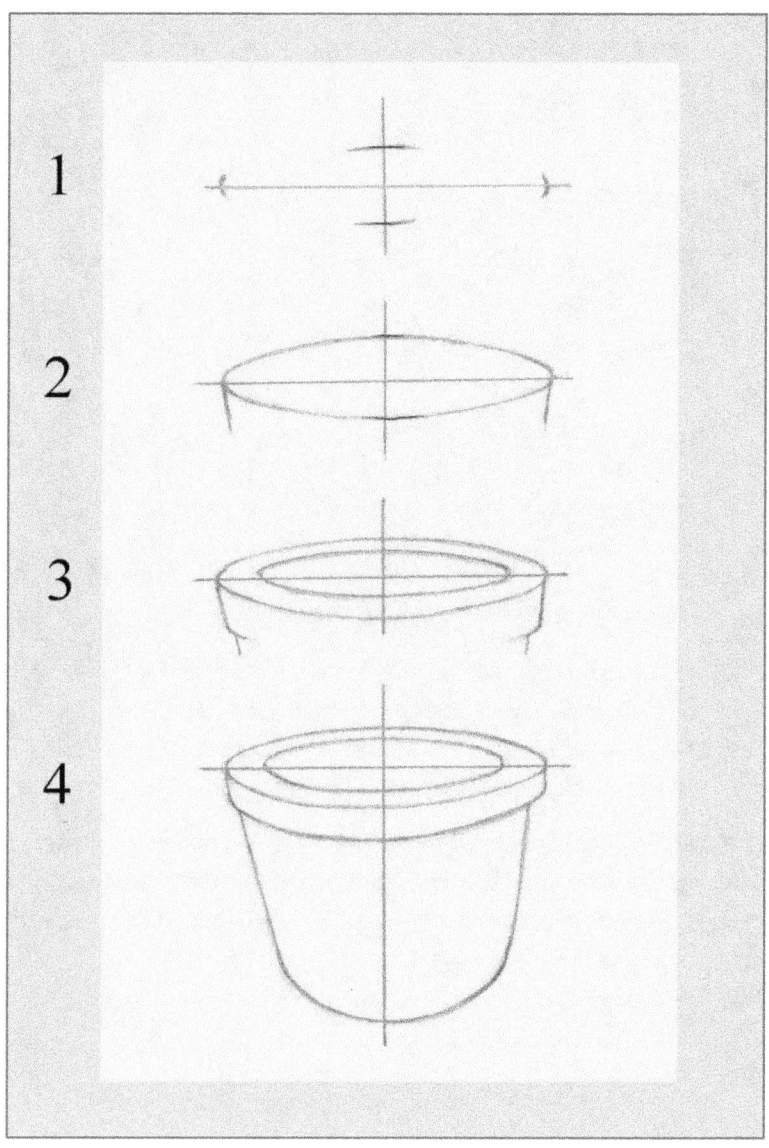

Depth of Ellipses

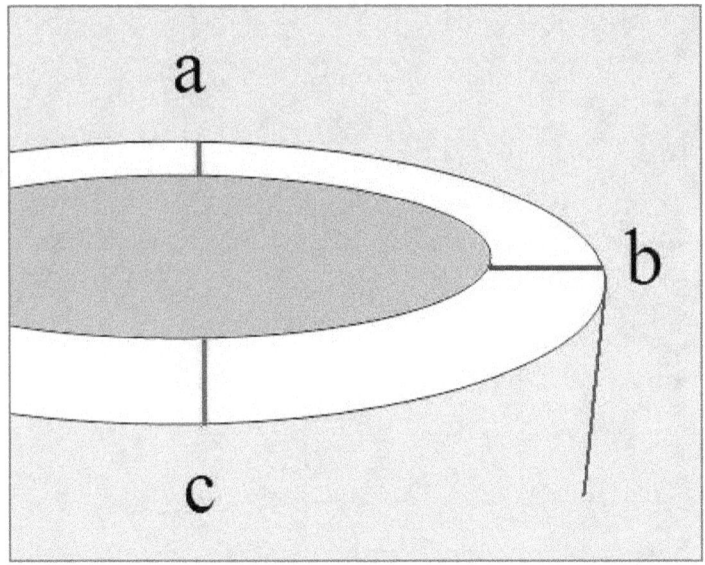

Observe the rim's depth which varies at different points of an ellipse.

Point **C** will appear wider than point **A**, since it is closer to the viewer. Point **B** will often appear wider than points **C** and **A** because of the foreshortening effect. Using this guide as the under-drawing will help when laying down highlights, shadows or detail on the vessel.

Once you are confident with drawing this hypothetical ellipse, try rendering real life ellipses, some of which might be multi-layered or threaded. Examples include bottle-tops, pepper-grinders, bowls, saucers, cups, jugs, teapot and decorative rings.

Glossary

Ambidextrous: Able to use the right or left hand equally.

Bilateral: Relating to two sides or affecting both sides.

Broca's Area: The part of the brain concerned with speech.

Composition: An artistically-arranged picture.

Corpus callosum: A network of nerve fibres connecting both hemispheres of the brain.

Dextral: Right-handed.

Ellipse: A symmetrical oval shape, often an oblique view of a cylindrical shape's top.

Lateral: Situated on one side or the other.

Negative space: Background shapes to objects.

Perspective: Representing a three-dimensional object onto a two-dimensional surface regarding its proportions and depth.

Positive shape: The subject matter as opposed to background.

Sinistral: Left-handed.

Roger W Sperry: psycho-biologist who discovered that the speech centre is located in the left brain and spacial awareness is in the right brain.

Vanishing point: A point where the outlines of a straight edge appear to converge on the horizon.

References

Books

DfES (2006) *Access for All* London: Department for Education and Skills

Edwards, B. (2001) *Drawing on the Right Side of the Brain (3rd Revised Edition)* London: HarperCollins

Gregory, R. L. (1987) *The Oxford Companion to the Mind* Oxford: Oxford University Press

Pinker, S. (1998) *How the Mind Works* London: The Penguin Press

Springer, S. P. and Duetsch, G. (1993) *Left Brain, Right Brain (4th edition)* New York: W H Freeman & Company

Zangwill, O. L. (1962) *Handedness and dominance* Baltimore: Reading Disabilities

Websites

www.bbc.co.uk: One Brain Two Halves

http://nobelprize.org: The Nobel Prize in Physiology or Medicine – 1981 Press Release

TV Programmes

Channel 5 *My Brilliant Brain* Broadcast 23.7.2007

Books by the Author

A graduate from Kingston University, Surrey and with a PCET teaching qualification from Warwick University, I have taught life drawing and have written numerous articles on teaching art.

This book has been inspired by my teaching experience and from my research into my other art assignments..

Art Books

Why do My Clouds Look Like Cotton Wool? – Plus 25 Solutions to Other Landscape Painting Peeves (Oil Painting Medic 2011)

Why do My Ellipses Look like Doughnuts? – Plus 25 Solutions to Other Still Life Painting Peeves (Oil Painting Medic 2011)

Landscape Painting in Oils: Twenty Step by Step Guides (Oil Painting Medic 2011)

The Artist's Garden in Oils: Eighteen Step by Step Guides (Oil Painting Medic 2012)

How Can I Inspire my Painting Class? (Lesson Plan Ideas for Oil Painting in Post Compulsory Education & an Essential Guide to Teaching) (Oil Painting Medic 2011)

Draw What You See, Not What You Think You See (Oil Painting Medic 2012)

Oil Paintings from Your Garden GMC Publications Ltd (2002)

Oil Paintings from the Landscape GMC Publications Ltd (2003)

Illustrated Children's Books

Katie's Magic Teapot and the Cosmic Pandas

Katie and the Cosmic Pandas' Deep Sea Voyage

Ben's Little Big Adventure